EDWARD PARTRIDGE

HARTT WIXOM

EDWARD PARTRIDGE

**The first bishop of
The Church of Jesus Christ of Latter-day Saints**

© 2010 Cedar Fort, Inc.

All rights reserved.

No part of this book may be reproduced in any form whatsoever, whether by graphic, visual, electronic, film, microfilm, tape recording, or any other means, without prior written permission of the publisher, except in the case of brief passages embodied in critical reviews and articles.

This is not an official publication of The Church of Jesus Christ of Latter-day Saints. The opinions and views expressed herein belong solely to the author and do not necessarily represent the opinions or views of Cedar Fort, Inc. Permission for the use of sources, graphics, and photos is also solely the responsibility of the author.

ISBN 13: 978-1-55517-362-3

Published by CFI, an imprint of Cedar Fort, Inc., 2373 W. 700 S., Springville, UT 84663
Distributed by Cedar Fort, Inc., www.cedarfort.com

Cover design and text layout by Corinne A. Bischoff
Cover design © 2010 by Lyle Mortimer

Printed in the United States of America

10 9 8 7 6 5 4 3 2 1

Printed on acid-free paper

About the Author

Hartt Wixom, 64, is the author of 12 books, both fiction and non-fiction, including *Hamblin*, the biography of Jacob Hamblin. He is also the author of hundreds of magazines articles and a lifetime of newspaper stories, many dealing with historical topics.

His newspaper training was in objective news reporting, the subject of his master's thesis at Brigham Young University. Besides a master's degree at BYU, he did post graduate work in history and English at the University of Utah, studying under veteran historians Davis Bitton, Charles Peterson, and David Miller. Wixom is a member of the Mormon History Assn.

As for the "objectivity" angle, Wixom said he debated for some time whether to disclose the fact he is a great, great grandson of Edward Partridge, via Edward Jr. "But I was determined to write it like I found it, no punches pulled. Fortunately, lengthy research indicates Edward and Lydia, as well as their children, despite a few human foibles, were devout Christians and Latter-day Saints. Desendants have a reason to be profoundly proud of the entire family."

Over the years, Wixom his received several regional and national awards for "unbiased writing" in the realm of investigative reporting.

The author and wife, Judene, Provo, are parents of seven children, Wendi, Julie, Wade, Peggy, Cindy, Jenny, Kamron.

Table of Contents

Acknowledgements		*viii*
Preface	Life and Legacy of Edward Partridge	*ix*
chapter one	"You are Impostors!"	1
chapter two	Stalwarts	13
chapter three	Mormon Concept of Zion	23
chapter four	Firestorm	43
chapter five	Steadying the Ark	69
chapter six	"The Solution to the Mormon Problem"	87
chapter seven	Tragedy and Triumph	101
chapter eight	The Legacy	117
	Sources Cited — Primary	138
	Sources Cited — Secondary	141
Appendices and Time Line		143
Index		173

Acknowledgements

Given what appeared a dearth of material about Edward Partridge, (perhaps one reason no in-depth biography had ever been published about him) all efforts to produce a book about the first bishop of the LDS Church appeared formidable indeed. Therefore, heart-felt acknowledgements are due many persons and institutions providing insightful information about what has been a rather enigmatic figure in LDS history.

In addition to sources listed at the end of each chapter in End Notes, I am particularly grateful to Carol Egbert, Layton, Utah, for valuable information obtained from Partridge descendants. Her husband, Gary, was also instrumental in meeting with sources.

Family news bulletins printed by the Edward Partridge family were also helpful. Unpublished local history was provided by Mr. and Mrs. Gordon F. Shipley, Oak City, Utah; also Bryant and Lyraine Jones, Provo, Utah, with affiliations to Oak City.

Grant Palmer, Sandy, Utah shared findings from extensive research he had conducted over the years about Mormon history. Dr. David J. Whitaker, curator, 19th Century Western and Mormon Americana at Brigham Young University, Provo, Utah, was helpful in locating primary sources, as was Bob Smead, Provo.

The work of Elder Larry K. Brown, Director, LDS Visitors Center, Independence, Mo., was appreciated in ferreting out vital LDS historical documents in Missouri. Ronald Romig, Reorganized LDS Church Archivist, Independence, Mo., assisted. Marilynn Barnes, Springfield, Mo., helped obtain data on the St. Louis Temple and events leading to its construction.

I am very grateful for records perused many times in BYU's Special Collections Office, and at the Library and Archives of the Church of Jesus Christ of Latter-day Saints, Salt Lake City, Utah, including the patience of historian James Kimball.

This book was greatly assisted by my wife, Judene, in researching genealogy, and data from secondary sources and from my mother, Adina Wixom, Salt Lake City, in conducting interviews with Partridge relatives. As always, Judene assisted in manuscript preparation.

This work would have been impossible, of course, without such primary sources as the diaries and journals maintained by the Partridge family members themselves.

They would seem to indicate the value in keeping accurate records of our own lives and of the history inevitably unfolding about us.

— *Hartt Wixom, Provo, Utah*

Preface

Life and Legacy of Edward Partridge

First Bishop of the LDS Church Edward Partridge..."was a pattern of piety, and one of the Lord's great men." — Joseph Smith's first mention of Edward in History of the Church.

Perhaps no man faced a greater challenge in the early days of the Church of Jesus Christ of Latter-day Saints, save Joseph Smith himself, than its first bishop, Edward Partridge. It was he who was sent by the Mormon prophet to establish the New Zion in Missouri. Little did either man likely know at the time what a firestorm of opposition awaited Edward in the discharge of his duties. Probably even Daniel of the Old Testament did not require more courage in the Lion's Den than did Edward in trying to acquire and distribute fairly Missouri lands for the saints in fulfillment of Doctrine and Covenants, Sect. 57.

Yet, in spite of his position as first bishop of the "Restored Church," the man labeled by Joseph Smith as a "pattern of piety...pure in heart, a man without guile as was Nathanael of Old," Edward died in relative obscurity in the early days of Nauvoo. For 157 years there was not even a grave marker placed over his burial site. It would seem that a man so prominent in LDS history just "dropped out of sight" and was forgotten. Edward Partridge, for whatever reason, has only recently begun to receive a modicum of the recognition he deserved during his life span of 46 years.

Since then, there have also been some negative comments about Bishop Partridge. He was "stubborn, defied the prophet, was too quiet, and yet fanatical in foisting his beliefs on others," etc. For years the world has known little about him, for Edward was not one to keep lengthy journals, nor tell us much about himself; he was an enigma even for many Latter-day Saints, as were his wife and children. But to know Edward Partridge and his family from Ohio to Utah, we must consider this insightful statement by Lucretia Lyman Ranney: "Without understanding their zeal to serve the Lord, you cannot understand the history of this family."

To explore fully Edward's role in LDS history, we must examine in particular his attempt to establish the Mormon Zion in hostile western Missouri. As history records, the Missourians would not tolerate in their midst the religious sect they called "Mormons." From Jackson to Clay, Van Buren, Ray,

Edward Partridge

Daviess and Caldwell counties, the saints were driven throughout the 1830s until it was clear any Mormon remaining west of the Mississippi River risked both property and life. With Gov. Lilburn Boggs' infamous "extermination order," it would appear that Joseph's vision of a Zion Utopia in the "Show-Me State" as well as Edward's commission to carry it out, lay in tatters.

At the outset, Partridge declared, "I must not fail." Did he, considering that by 1839 no Latter-day Saint dared remain in the "Promised Land"? What exactly was his role as first LDS bishop under the Prophet Joseph Smith in the Restored Church? What insights might we gain from the efforts of Edward Partridge to bring us greater success in our own endeavors to be more Christ-like?

What, too, might we learn from Lydia, his wife, and their children? Lydia never wavered in her faith despite many hardships following Edward's death, the Nauvoo expulsion and difficult trek to Utah. Lydia also played a little-known role in following the directive of President Brigham Young in selling the LDS temple lot site in Independence, Mo. to raise money for the exodus to Utah.

The entire Partridge family seemed to have had a "spiritual grit" about them which all Latter-day Saints, indeed, all who worship the Divine Being, might do well to emulate. How they acquired the same could guide many of us in our own lives.

chapter one

"You are Impostors!"

The four young men at the door on this autumn day in 1830 seemed earnest enough. They wore the look of crusading zeal, claiming they had something for Edward that he and his wife would value highly: the restored gospel of Jesus Christ as found on Earth during the time of the Savior in the Meridian of Times. They had come from Fayette, Seneca County, New York and talked of a new church organized there by the "prophet" Joseph Smith April 6 of that year.[1]

The entire message seemed most presumptuous to Edward. He had not become a successful hatter and businessman in Painesville, Ohio by being naive nor undisciplined in matters of either heart or mind. In fact, it was clear from his meticulously kept business records (those we have) that he was a master of fine details; acquaintances said he had a retentive mind from which very little escaped.

To be true, Edward sought most earnestly to better know God's will. He and his wife, Lydia, had often searched through prayer and study to know whether the Campbellite faith they had recently joined pleased God. With Sidney Rigdon as minister, the members were known as "Disciples" in an apparent effort to follow Christ. But the Partridges sought something more spiritually fulfilling, something which fathomed deeper than surface worship, something which warmed their inward souls and made them feel closer to their Maker. Most of all, they sought to know what God would have them do to serve Him.

Historian B. H. Roberts wrote that, "Nothing worthy of note transpired in his youth, with this exception, that he remembered...that the Spirit of the Lord strove with him a number of times insomuch that his heart was made tender and he went and wept; and sometimes he went silently and poured the effusions of his soul to God in prayer...At the age of 20, he had become disgusted with the religious world. He saw no beauty, comeliness or loveliness in the character of God as represented by the teachings of the various religious sects."[2]

Roberts says Edward heard a Universal Restorationer preach upon the love of God and concluded that the sermon seemed reasonably accurate according to the Bible. He and Lydia accepted the "Campbellite" religion "even though doubting at times it being the true one..."[3]

Edward's mind had rarely been idle upon the subject of religion. He had rejected much of orthodox belief. But he kept an open mind in a relentless quest for religious truth and expressed the hope that some day he would find it in the purity and simplicity of the Savior's reign on Earth. As Edward himself put it, he "did not, as have many under like circumstances, discard the Bible and lose faith in the Supreme Being because of the shortcomings of those who professed to worship Him...he was satisfied that God lived, that the touchstone [was] to try the teachings of the ministers and professors with whom he came in contact."[4]

But how could these men babbling at the door possibly be true messengers of Heaven? They did not talk about the Christian Bible at all but a new scripture called the Book of Mormon. Indeed, the *Bible* had sufficed for thousands of years. Why did the world suddenly need more than a Bible? He did take note they exhibited a certain sincerity and warmth. Giving their names as Oliver Cowdery, Parley P. Pratt, Peter Whitmer and Ziba Petersen, they looked, however, like many others who had been crying across the countryside, "Lo here is God, lo there!" Edward had seen fervent religious revivalists all the way to New York and back. These men seemed to be just another example of spiritual fervor sweeping the nation. No, Edward would continue to pray and study in the hope that some day God would answer his prayers and reveal to him and his wife the true religion they so earnestly sought. He must be patient.

Edward told the men boldly, to their faces, that he believed them to be "impostors." Nevertheless, an undaunted Cowdery bore a powerful testimony. He "was thankful that there was a God in Heaven who knew the hearts of all men." According to Lydia's diary, the testimony seemed to have a delayed impact on Edward, for she wrote: "After the men were gone, my husband sent a man to follow them up and get one of their books."[5]

After reading the Book of Mormon, Lydia was readily converted and soon baptized by Elder Parley P. Pratt. She said she believed because, "I saw the gospel in its plainness, as it was in the New Testament, and I also knew that none of the sects of the day taught those things."[6] She and Edward were in the habit of making important decisions together. In this matter, she must have thought her husband would soon follow.

But Edward needed more convincing. He must have a talk with this Joseph Smith. According to historian Dean Jessee, Edward finally found him. "Arriving in Manchester, New York, Edward found the Smith family had moved, but...he inquired among neighbors about their character. He located Joseph preaching at a meeting in his father's house in Waterloo. When the Prophet invited comment from listeners, Edward arose and stated that he had been to Manchester, had observed the 'good order and industry' exhibited at the Smith farm, noticed the sacrifices they had made for the sake of their faith, and having discovered that the Smith character was questioned upon no other point than that of their religion, [Joseph's 'Golden Bible'] Edward requested immediate baptism at the hands of the prophet. Edward's request was granted the following day, being baptized Dec. 11, 1830, in the Seneca River by Joseph himself. Being baptized by immersion, as revealed repeatedly to the saints through Bible and Book of Mormon, required no little faith and courage considering the adverse factors of ice and cold in the Seneca River at that time of year. Edward would need that faith and courage, for almost from the time he joined the Church of Jesus Christ of Latter-day Saints, Partridge appeared targeted, even more than usual, to be tested by the fury of Satan's forces.

But at last Edward felt he could anchor his soul and root his will in a faith to please God.

Much has been written in church history about the Smith family being characterized as something other than people of integrity and citizenship, but if so, Edward's scrutiny found the opposite. In hearing Joseph preach, Edward had the opportunity to make up his own mind about the man claiming to have talked with God and Christ in the Sacred Grove in the spring of 1820.

. Edward found nothing contrary to the truth which he so diligently sought. He also saw that this new religion was not based on "mysticism, "intellectualism" or some vague inspiration as were other churches. Joseph claimed to see and hear with his own two eyes and ears immortal God and Christ as two separate, glorified beings in the likeness and image of man.[7]

The concept of God and Christ as two distinct beings in glorified human form was an iconoclasm for those days; both Catholics and Protestants believed in the Nicene Creed.[8] Yet, the concept conformed to Edward and Lydia's long-held beliefs; it seemed true to Genesis 1:26, *Let us make man in our image, after our likeness.* The testimony of young Smith that he had been guided by an angel over a period of four years to obtain metal plates containing a history of God's dealings with the American Indians and translate them by the gift and power of God was, indeed, something new. But it did not contradict what they already believed in; rather it seemed to add to their previous concept of God. Then, too, there was that scripture in Revelations 14:6: "And I saw another angel fly in the midst of Heaven, having the everlasting gospel to preach to them that dwell on the earth..."

True, the claim to have new scripture was new to Edward and Lydia; but when one read the Book of Mormon, it did seem in harmony with the Bible, and to be precisely what it claimed: an account of God's dealings with the aborigine of America. Was not the "Indian" one of God's children? Did not Christ in John 10:16 tell the Israelites in Judea that he had "other sheep not of this fold...and they shall hear my voice"? Who were those other sheep if not the people elsewhere, perhaps of another continent? The Book of Mormon revealed to investigators the story of the "Lamanites" or follower of Laman, who came to America at the time of severe persecution of the Jews in Jerusalem about 600 B.C. In accepting the Book of Mormon, the Partridges were satisfied that it accounted for the Indians being present in America when Columbus arrived. It apparently seemed logical to Edward and Lydia that God should care about these people, give them commandments as He did the Children of Israel on the other side of the world, and that the commandments written down on metal plates, might well constitute scripture as recorded in the Book of Mormon. The story of the book's miraculous coming forth, i. e. the last record-keeper in the book being one Moroni who revealed to Joseph the location of the plates over a period of four years, would certainly require deep meditation and prayer. But if the Partridges were looking for God's hand to be revealed in the latter days, what more significant claim than this? If there were prophets in olden times, why could the Lord not raise one in modern times? Was a prophet not needed? And why limit God's power to ancient Israel?

The claims of this new church were clear and forthright in knowing the "true and everlasting God" as explained in John 17:3. Although the claim to be "God's one and only true church," was somewhat overwhelming, yet how could a church be...if not claiming to be?

Shortly after being introduced to Edward, the Prophet Joseph Smith says this of him in the (Documentary) History of the Church, p. 218: "In December, Sidney Rigdon came to inquire of the Lord, and with him came Edward Partridge; the latter was a pattern of piety and one of the Lord's great men. He is a man without guile as was Nathanael of old." This referred to the Gospel of John in the New Testament. After Nathanael recognized Jesus as "Rabbi...the Son of God," Jesus hailed Nathanael as "an Israelite without guile."[9]

The Lord must have just been waiting for Edward to be baptized. Shortly afterward, as given in D&C Section 36, Joseph recorded the Lord's voice to Edward as follows: "...you are called to preach my gospel as with the voice of a trump...the Holy Ghost shall teach you the peaceable things of the kingdom and you shall share it with a loud voice, saying Hosanna, blessed be the name of the most High God."

Although Joseph was surrounded by many great men in his lifetime, including Brigham Young, Heber C. Kimball, Wilford Woodruff, John Taylor et al, the prophet has no higher praise than for Edward Partridge. The prophet's appreciation and affection for Edward would grow. Some church members would be elevated to high stations, such as Rigdon, yet few seemed closer to the prophet's heart throughout his lifetime than Partridge. This can be seen from the continued trust placed in Edward to hold the saints' money and disperse property to them fairly.

The Partridges had acquired many material goods prior to joining the Restored Church, as indicated by daughter Eliza. She says that when Mormonism found her family, they had a most comfortable home, with shop and barn, two lots adjoining the Public Square, and a 20-acre wood lot next to town. The Partridge abode in Painesville (not far from Kirtland, Ohio) was equipped with "large living quarters, food storage rooms, a front yard with green plat, rosebushes, a well with an old oaken bucket, currant bushes, a summer home with grapes, flowers, paths, and many arbor vines."[10] They were to give it all up for the gospel.

What was it in Edward and Lydia's makeup, background and upbringing that would make it possible for them to willingly forsake so much for a spiritual cause they believed in?

Let us look into the background of these two to see what might have shaped them to be the sort of Latter-day Saints they became. Edward was born to William and Jemima Partridge (see genealogy chart) Aug. 27, 1793 in Pittsfield, Massachusetts. By that time, the Partridges had settled on the above spelling of their last name, although if one was to trace their genealogy, they would find it had been Patrigg, Patrick and Patreck.[11] Edward's forefathers had embraced the Presbyterian faith in England and Scotland. His grandfather was a member of the "Solemn Covenanter" who had bound themselves in a series of agreements or covenants to uphold the tenets of Calvin, in protest of Roman Catholic restrictions on Bible study and worship according to conscience.[12]

Most of the Partridge clan had, like that of Joseph Smith's family, been devout believers in deity, although not always happy with orthodox Christianity. Edward's parents seemed to have instilled in their son a desire to acquire truth and live in harmony with it. That appeared to be the most important value system in the lives of both Edward and Lydia.

One event which helped shaped Edward's religious beliefs was when he "heard a Universal Restorationer preach upon the love of God."[13] He seemed attracted to that concept of deity, as opposed to the "fire and brimstone" preachments of many ministers of the day. Interestingly, while Edward had frequently found fault with those preaching Christianity, he never did so, at least openly, with Joseph Smith as prophet of the Restoration.

Historian D. Brent Collette says that Edward came by his "religious bent" quite naturally in that many of his ancestors were ministers, and well educated ones at that.[14] Edward's mother, Jemima, was a daughter of Rev. Adonijah Bidwell, a graduate of Yale University, and granddaughter of Rev. Ebenizer Devotion, a graduate of Harvard. Edward's grandmother, Anna Partridge, was the daughter of Rev. William Williams. Edward's sister married a minister. In joining the Mormons, Edward rejected much that his family had long cherished, including the concept of God, Christ and Holy Ghost as members of the (three in one) Trinity. Still, the value of living a spiritual life seems to be an ingrained concept that Edward inherited or embraced with devotion and conviction as had his immediate ancestors.

Looking at Edward's life from a temporal perspective, he had been ambitious and diligent in the hatter's trade, serving early as an apprentice in New York State. During that era, beaver hats were in fashion which required considerable artistic and mechanical skills. Men were willing to pay up to $20, a nice sum in those days, for headwear fashioned from the properly skinned and cured beaver "fuzz" (not the heavy fur) which was both water resistant and long-wearing. With some 12 pelts required to make a single hat, all must be meshed tightly together to make a top grade hat. Edward does not tell us if he specialized as a milliner in women's hats or men's headgear. But he must have been very good at his profession, for he prospered materially. Edward soon bought out a partner and moved his trade to Painesville, Ohio, just east of present-day Cleveland. One of Edward's journals tell of a lengthy trip to conduct hattery business in the Great Lakes area and possibly to buy beaver pelts, which were usually sold on the frontier water ports.[15] After joining the Mormons, Edward seemed to transform much of his business acumen and energies into the Restored Church. The hattery trade was forgotten.

Lydia's background carries a strong hint of Biblical influence. Her father's name was Joseph and four generations back carried the name Ezekial.[16] Her background was filled with stubborn adherence to principle amid affluence and nobility. Her family came originally from Normandy (France) and when William the Conqueror invaded and defeated England in 1066, three of her ancestors were cited for valor by William following the Battle of Hastings. The DeClisbe (as it was then known) family was granted title and lands in England for some 600 years and were held in high esteem in the courts of various kings. However, in 1642, the then king of England demanded a pledge of submission from the family which two of the DeClisbe family refused to give. Rather than submit to the arbitrary dictum of a "selfish, unconstitutional court," the men elected to leave the country forever. They were heavily fined and their property confiscated. They immediately set sail for the colonial province of New York. Later, the court which reprimanded the family was severely censured by calmer heads in England and the Clisbees (as they were now known) were granted lands "the width of the states" of New York and Connecticut by a Royal Commission from King Charles.[17] Lydia's family later moved to Massachusetts where many of her family members became carpenters and builders.

Interestingly, the Clisbees showed their loyalty to the new land of America in the Revolutionary War by fighting against England. Lydia's grandfather Ezekial was a Minute Man for the colonies.

Family unity was strong among the Clisbees. At age 22, Lydia's mother died and with other family members she moved to northeastern Ohio to be near her mother's family. Lydia's dedication to family ties showed strongly in the Restored Church she had just joined, remaining close to daughters and a son even decades after her husband died.

Despite many attempts, Edward did not in an entire lifetime of trying ever convince any of his family members to join with him in the Restored Gospel. Lydia says that Edward's family "treated him coldly," as he attempted to convert them to his new faith, and thought him "deranged in mind." When it came time for him to depart for home, one of his brothers, James Harvey, was sent with Edward, "and stayed awhile with us and was baptized." But, says Lydia, he later turned from the Church and "denied ever being baptized."[18]

As a member of the Campbellite Church, Lydia says, "We had much happiness." After joining the Mormons, blessings came, sure enough, but only after many hardships. Lydia says in her journal that about the time a daughter came down with a serious illness "...My husband was called by revelation to go with a number of others to Missouri to locate a place for the gathering of the saints;

the unbelievers thought he must be crazy or he would not go. I thought I had reason to think my trials had commenced, and so [they] had, but this trial like all others was followed with blessings, for our daughter recovered."[19]

When Mormonism found Partridge, it also found the pastor of Edward's Campbellite church, Sidney Rigdon, in Mentor, Ohio near Kirtland. P. P. Pratt had been a member of Sidney's Campbellite congregation and testified to Rigdon about the "Restoration of all things" and showed him a Book of Mormon. Rigdon was so impressed he brought his entire Campbellite flock, numbering some 1,000 souls, into the Mormon faith. Rigdon soon traveled to see the young Mormon prophet and give him the good news.[20] Sidney managed to persuade Smith to look into moving the church from western New York, where persecution was growing, to Kirtland. He did so in December, 1830, eight months after the church was organized in Fayette, New York.

In the years which followed, the lives of Edward and Sidney would be much intertwined. Rigdon remained steadfast to the church during times of "fair weather," but Partridge remained unshakeable to the end against all adversity. Edward seemed to have taken the attitude that once making the decision to be baptized, one does not bail out when the going gets tough. Joseph could not have had a more loyal friend than Edward Partridge for the remainder of the latter's life, even when Rigdon and other church leaders would desert the prophet.

Remaining loyal became more difficult after the church moved enmasse from the Kirtland area to Missouri. Elders Pratt, Cowdery, Whitmer and Petersen had taken their missionary labors to Missouri, and found it a fertile land for Lamanite converts, as well as for growing crops. According to LDS writer Robert Mullen, the missionaries found Native Americans "eager to learn about the Book of Mormon, a sparsely-settled land with good soil...and an opportunity to form a new society after their own ideas."[21] The missionaries took their glowing report to Joseph Smith at Kirtland where some 2,000 Mormons had by now gathered.

On June 19, 1831, Joseph began a long journey across the breadth of Ohio, Indiana and Illinois and across the state of Missouri to have a look for himself at the western edge of the

United States, "near the borders of the Lamanites." Joseph took along the following in the order listed by him: Sidney Rigdon, Martin Harris, Edward Partridge, W. W. Phelps, Joseph Coe, Algernon S. Gilbert, and his wife.[22] "I started from Kirtland, Ohio, for the land of Missouri, agreeable to the commandment before received [D&C 52:2-5] wherein it was promised that if we were faithful, the land of our inheritance, even the place for the city of the New Jerusalem, should be revealed."[23]

The events which followed would have a profound impact on the life of Edward and Lydia Partridge in ways neither could likely have foreseen.

end notes, chapter one

1. B. H. Roberts, editor, adds this footnote to the *Documentary History of the Church* (DHC) by Joseph Smith, 1:129.
2. Ibid.
3. Ibid. See also unpublished "Long Journal of Edward Partridge," LDS Church Archives, Salt Lake City, UT. Compiled by Edward Partridge Jr., Fillmore, UT, 1878.
4. Partridge Family Bulletin, August 1954, No. 4, pp. 1, 2
5. Lydia Partridge, "Long Journal of Edward Partridge," p. 6. This was likely written in Lydia's later years. She is not known to have kept a daily diary during the Missouri period.
6. Historian Dean Jessee, "Steadfastness and Patient Endurance: the Legacy of Edward Partridge," p. 3. See also June, 1979 issue of *Ensign* magazine, published by the Church of Jesus Christ of Latter-day Saints.
7. There is nothing in writing in official LDS church history indicating Joseph Smith taught openly the concept of God and Christ as separate, physical (glorified) beings prior to his *History of the Church* in 1838. (He had been commanded to begin keeping a written record upon organization of the church in 1830.)

    But evidence points to his teaching the principle well before 1838. See *History of Joseph Smith* by his mother, Lucy Mack Smith, p. 82; *BYU Studies, Spring,* pp. 278-79; "Kirtland Letter Book," 1829-35. pp. 1-6; "Palymyra Reflector," Feb. 14, 1831. The latter date coincedes with the approximate time Edward Partridge joined the church.

With the First Vision occurring in the spring of 1820, this may seem a long time before recording the same. Perhaps a prophet, especially a young one, needs time to reflect upon the gravity of a heavenly vision. For example, the Apostle Paul did not record his "First Vision" experienced on the road to Damascus (Acts 22:6-8) in 35 A.D. until some 20 years later; it is first mentioned in Gal. 1:15-16, so far as we have record.

8. The Nicene Creed, believed by many Catholics and Protestants even today, holds that God and Christ are of "one substance" and that God the Father "was made flesh, was made man...and rose on the third day." The creed was not formulated from any eyewitness claim, but from members of a political convention in Nicea, 325 A.D., called by the Emperor Constantine. Source: *World Book Encyclopedia*, Vol. N, p. 318.

9. See John 1:45-51. Through the power of the Holy Ghost, Nathanael knew Christ for what he was, as did Peter in the last days of the Savior's ministry. Note: the spelling of Nathanael appears here as it does in the King James version of the New Testament. It is not the same spelling used in some latter-day references.

10. Edward Partridge Family Bulletin, August 1957, p. 1.

11. Lucretia Lyman Ranney, *Our Priceless Heritage*, Part II, "American Ancestry of Edward Partridge" p. 1.

12. *World Book Encyclopedia*, Vol. Ci-Cz, p. 885.

13. Roberts, DHC, footnotes, 1:129.

14. Collette, Master's thesis, BYU, "In Search of Zion," p.15

15. "The Journal of Edward Partridge, 1818," Examine early pages.

16. Ranney, Part II, "American Ancestry of Lydia Clisbee," pp. 1-2.

17. Ibid.

18. Lydia Partridge, unpublished diary, p. 6, "Long Journal of Edward Partridge."

19. Ibid.

20. Robert Mullen, *The Latter-day Saints Yesterday, Today and Tomorrow*, p. 31.

21. Ibid.

22. Joseph Smith had by this time selected Sidney Rigdon as his first counselor, usually putting him first when listing names. There is apparently no other meaning in the order of names listed. The name of Gilbert's wife is not given.

23. DHC 1:188.

chapter two

Stalwarts

One thing is clear about new converts Edward and Lydia Partridge. They had made a commitment. They would live up to it. An example of this in Edward's life is his letter to his parents after they had rebuffed his initial attempt to convert them to the Restored Gospel. The letter also gives us a glimpse of the man's strength and faith toward the new Church of Jesus Christ of Latter-day Saints, as well as his compassion for his family.

He begins,[1] "Honored Father and Mother and Beloved Brothers and Sisters...it is with a degree of deference that I sit down to address this letter to you upon the all important subject of the Christian religion, but having felt for some time that it was my duty, I cheerfully yield to the dictates of my own conscience hoping to give no offence (sic) even if I should appear in the character of a teacher.

"...few at the present day realize that the hand of the Lord is visible in the things that are transpiring around us...I assure you I am not deluded neither am I deceived, for having had sufficient time and opportunity to examine and compare the Book of Mormon, and the revelations given direct to us, with the Bible and the doings of God in other ages, I find they are in unison, and not only that but the prophecies that are fulfilling in this our day are so striking that I wonder that every discerning person is not convinced of the truth of this work."

At this point Edward explains why more than a Bible is needed in the latter days. He quotes the 31st page of the Book of Mormon, "Blessed are they which shall seek to bring forth my Zion at that day, for they shall receive the gift and power of the Holy Ghost." No doubt Edward's traditionalist Protestant forebears were well acquainted with all the promises of a Zion in the last days but

Edward is asking where is the evidence, or even the claim of Zion being established in the latter days — other than the church he has just joined? As for "Gift and power of the Holy Ghost," Edward adds this powerful testimony: "...there are hundreds if not thousands who can bear testimony to the gifts of the spirit being in this church, such as speaking in tongues, healing the sick, discerning of spirits, casting out devils etc."

Edward and Lydia would give credit to this witness of the spirit, of course, for sustaining them in their tumultuous first few years in the new church. But to William and Jemima and their family, Edward's fervent testimony, not in his parents' direct realm of experience, may have seemed as babbling. So too might have Edward's rehearsing of the wickedness and vanity and unbelief of those who oppose the Lord's true church in the latter days. But Edward writes on undaunted. For some 16 pages in his letter, Edward quotes both Bible and Book of Mormon prophecies, and states that many of them are fulfilled in the church of the Mormons. He asks his parents, "Notwithstanding you are honest unto men, are you honest to God in all things? Have ye a conscience void of offence before him?"

Then comes this poignant line: "I can assure you it is not a trifling thing to give up all for Christ's sake, to be willing to even lay down our lives in his cause." Edward expresses the hope that "...in eternity we may meet in the Celestial Kingdom of God to spend eternity in his presence." He concludes the letter by saying, "I hope you will not be offended at me, for my zeal in trying to convince you of the religion I profess...I remain in the bonds of your love." (Signed Edward Partridge.)

In the few pictures available of Edward, he is an imposing figure, a tall man with dark hair, high cheek bones, a countenance of stern yet smiling patience. Those who knew him well could likely see in the portrait a man ready to do all in his humanly power to be counted worthy of the Savior's trust. The above letter would indicate that Edward was tall in spiritual devotion as well as physical appearance. It is clear Edward was fully committed to the latter-day work. People knew where he stood.

Edward's letters also showed deep compassion for his family, whether parents or wife and children. A typical letter to Lydia begins, "My Dear Wife..."[2] His penchant for details is there: "I expect the house will not be finished until toward spring...they are preparing to commence plastering soon. As to the amount of corn you will want..." Endearment is always manifest: "I have had great anxiety for two or three days past to be with you, to comfort and take care of you..." To his daughter, he wrote, "Harriet my daughter, it rejoices me to have you write me..."[3]

Quite likely, it was this selfless "piety" as Joseph Smith put it (defined in *The American Heritage Dictionary* as "Religious devotion and reverence" to God and/or family) which led to Edward being called as First (ordained) Bishop of the Church. Although the prophet had known Edward for only two months, Edward was called to the important office of first bishop of the Restoration with these words in D&C 41:9, "And I have called my servant Edward Partridge and give a commandment, that he should be...ordained a bishop unto the church...to "leave his merchandise and to spend all his time in the labors of the church."

There followed this letter issued by Joseph, Oliver Cowdery, W. W. Phelps, John Whitmer and Sidney Rigdon:

> "We hereby certify that Edward Partridge, bishop of the church of the Latter-day Saints [along with Isaac Morley] are personally known to us, having been faithful members of the church from its first organization in this state, and as men of piety, veracity and strict moral principles and virtues, we recommend them to all...we know they have been tried with affliction and adversity, persecutions and peril for the sake of the religion which they have espoused...and should any man of like faith be disposed to entrust moneys or other propertys [sic] in their hands for the good of the poor and afflicted or for any other purpose, they will find them to be perfectly honest and strictly responsible."[4]

But lest the reader suppose that Edward had no foibles whatsoever in the attempt to know him better, let it be said there were idiosyncrasies. One thing Edward seemed to be derelict in was keeping a daily record of his activities during the critical period of the latter-day Restitution of all Things. In all of religious history following the sojourn of the Savior on Earth, probably no period was more important to keep meticulous records than that immediately following Joseph Smith's claim to receive heavenly messages from God and Christ. Edward Jr. would later scold his father for not having kept more journals during his lifetime. (Edward Jr. wrote nine lengthy journals covering thousands of pages and intimate thoughts on nearly every gospel subject. This is apparently what he had in mind for his father that the world might know him better, as well as the faithful manner in which Edward Sr. discharged his church duties.) The journals that Edward Sr. did keep were, as mentioned, meticulous in details during the period he wrote, but there were gaps. From his baptism in 1830 to the missionary journey of 1835-37, and afterward, he is mostly silent.

At one time, Edward failed to account for $29 entrusted to him. He admitted the same in his account to a conference of saints and they told him he needn't worry about it. He was handling thousands of dollars in his duties as bishop and he had already gained such a reputation for honesty that they forgave him for it. In fact, much money was delivered into the hands of Partridge. At one point Oliver Cowdery brought him some $3,000 from the saints in Ohio for the "building up of the kingdom."[5] But there is no indication after not accounting for the $29 that he ever failed to account for every penny of church money.

The saints in Ohio were also instructed by Joseph Smith to send all business transactions dealing with church matters to Partridge even though he was in Missouri. This would be consistent with Edward's being bishop, but the same occurred even after Newell K. Whitney had been designated bishop in Ohio. Apparently, Edward was still bishop of the entire church and as such would be expected to balance the church's books in a land 1,000 miles away. Says historian H. S. Partridge, "Thus the long-suffering bishop in Missouri was to be made responsible for debts of the saints in Ohio."[6]

Another "fault" of Edward's, at least before being converted to Mormonism, was writing what can only be called dreadfully dull prose. For example, the journal of a business trip to Michigan contains entries such as the following:

> "On the 25th of April 1818, I left Painesville for Mackinous. Sunday 26th, went on board in the morn...at evening hoisted sail under a light land breeze. Monday 27th, little or no wind.

> Tuesday, 28th, wind rose anchor off Cleveland...wind on shore at evening hauled a little more favorable so we weighed anchor and the next morn Wednesday 29th were off...we lay at Detroit till the next Friday during which time there were very high winds attended with snow and rain, one of the most sudden changes of wind I ever knew happened...while we lay here the wind blew apparently a gale up the river...on a sudden it died away and in the course of half a minute it blew equally as hard..."[7]

He later provides in great detail the ice conditions on Lake Huron. There is no mention of his thoughts or philosophies during this time. Quite likely, this 1818 journal reflected a period when he was not particularly concerned with life outside routine business transactions.

Of course, wind conditions and weather were extremely important to anyone traveling by sail in the early 1800s, the only form of large boat conveyance. Still, these entries seem to be the reflections of a man focused on the physical world, with little contemplation beyond the here and now. Journal entries become much more animated in 1835 when Edward details a mission he took eastward. He seems to have found new purpose in life:[8] "About noon we arrived in Lexington, LaFayette Co. We tried for a meeting but found that they did not wish to hear...we also tried where we lodged the night before...crossed a 12 mile prairie but could not get a meeting, traveled in all 15 miles and was kindly entertained by a Mr. J. Hall among the Cumberland Presbyterians...the 5th, read the scriptures and in the evening preached at brother S's upon the subject of blessings...The 23rd I preached in the school house to an attentive congregation...shouting Hosanna, blessed be the name of the most high God."[9]

Edward's patriarchal blessing, given him by Joseph Smith Sr. because Edward "had no father" who could give him one, includes lines such as this:

> Bro. Partridge, let thy heart sink down in humility, give thyself up into the hands of thy God and be willing to receive the blessings that is he is willing to bestow upon thee...thou art a chosen man of God, who did look upon thee before the foundation of the world and has set thee apart to do good to his cause...the Lord will bless thee with the ministrations of Angels,

because of the integrity of thy heart, and thy willingness to obey His commandments. Thou art one of the horns of Joseph that are to push the people together, from the ends of the earth. Thou heart shall be enlarged from this very hour! Thou shalt have great wisdom to execute thy mission and callings. Thou shalt perform great miricles [sic] and shall have faith even like unto the brother of Jared. Thy wife shall be blessed also and receive the desire of her heart. She shall have night visions and thereby know of thy welfare in thy absence.[10]

Edward is then promised, even though never being known as powerful of tongue (compared to golden-throated orator Sidney Rigdon) that he shall "have great power to speak beyond anything of which thou hast thought." He was also told that he shall stand in his office [as bishop of the church] "until thou art weary of it and shall desire to resign it."

It may not have taken long for the latter to come about. Not only did Edward have to contend with Missouri enemies outside the church but brethren within who may have disagreed with the phrase, "according to need." Surely it would require an "enlargement" of his heart, as the blessing specified, to overlook some of the problems carried with him to his bedroom every night. Novelist Ruth Louise Partridge says that Edward "grew thin and hollow-eyed and could never be sure his sleep wouldn't be broken by the importuning of some saint."[11] Both Edward and Lydia were nothing if not charitable. When a widow with four children had no place to live, the Partridges took in the family even though it now meant "12 or 13 living in a one-room cabin."[12] It was said of Edward that when some of his own family's long-awaited material goods arrived from Ohio that he placed them in the storehouse for needy poor who should soon be on hand.[13] Did family members first give their approval? There is nothing in the record to so indicate.

His daughters would later hint that Edward carried the virtue of charity to a fault.[14]

But he would be one of "Joseph's" horns, as stated in his patriarchal blessing, to push people together from ends of the earth."[15] He would be the ramrod of the church to see that temporal affairs were expedited for the material and spiritual welfare of the saints.

One example of Edward's trials in administering his office of bishop regarding dispersement of lands is indicated in a letter he wrote to Joseph Smith in November 1833 from Jackson County after the saints had been driven from their homes by mobs: "...many are living in tents and shanties...We are in hopes we will be able to return to our houses and lands before a great while, but how this is to be accomplished is all in the dark to us as yet. Some of our brethren who have given me money to buy land with are desirous to receive a deed of some land and I have thought it best to give deeds to such as are anxious to have them. I want your advice on this subject in this time of trial."[16]

Apparently, Edward decided not to give out individual deeds to lands purchased for the incoming saints but rather write out leasing papers only. This way the property would remain in common for the poor of the church if the original participant defaulted, or was excommunicated.

Edward was not specifically instructed, however, what to do if the member left the church and then took his claim to Missouri's civil courts. State law would supercede church law. It was just one of the many temporal matters he would have to worry about as bishop. What, indeed, was fair to both individual and church? And what would hold up in Missouri courts?

Then there is the matter of deciding just who was poor. It appears Edward didn't want to bother the prophet in many mundane matters, but he was in Missouri witnessing the saints' problems more intensely than those not present. He had to make decisions based on what he daily witnessed, while someone might interpret the same as taking too much authority on himself without waiting for specific instruction from the prophet.

While Edward was said to be a "practical man" (a reason he was selected as a leader in temporal affairs), he was also an idealist and poet, especially about the concept of Zion, expressing the deeper spiritual values of heaven in several ways. An insight can be seen in examining lines of this song now included in LDS Hymn Books:[17] "Let Zion in her beauty rise [title of song] Her Light begin to shine. Ere long her King will rend the skies, Majestic and divine. The Gospel spreading through the land, A people to prepare...To meet the Lord and Enoch's band, Triumphant in the air." Other lines from his song: "That Jesus in the clouds above, With hosts of angels too, Will soon appear, his Saints to save, His enemies subdue."

Edward proclaims in the song that prophets foretell the return of Zion and then: "Dear Lord, prepare my heart To Stand with thee on Zion's mount And never more to part..." (For complete words to song, see Appendix B). Edward early caught the vision of Zion in the Restoration of all Things and what its return to Earth would mean to the saints. He did not see all the yearnings of his song come to pass on this Earth, but they are presented here to better comprehend the magnitude of his thinking on the subject of man's relationship to God. And the different man he became after joining the latter day movement.

As any English teacher can attest, he knew, or learned something about the eloquence of words, rhythm and meter. He shows an artistic nature in these verses for which, lamentably, he was little known during his lifetime.

Another of Edward's songs reads:[18] "O may our minds be drawn away From Worldly cares just now...That we may worship thee our God While at thy feet we bow...O let thy blessings shower around By day and also night...Not only us but all thy saints who in thy law delight."

An insight into the man's faith, indeed, his positive attitude, can be seen from his journal comments upon returning home from a long mission: "I arrived at my family about 5 p.m. [during difficult times in Clay County, Mo.] and found them well. I think I shall be thankful as I ever did, in being permitted to again rejoin my family."[19] They could not have been "well" materially at this time. But, as usual, Edward applied a spiritual, not a material yardstick.

Edward's prayers, particularly during the trying Missouri period, would prove his personal insight into matters of the spirit. One begins, "Oh Lord look down in mercy upon thy people, who are afflicted and oppressed. How long O Lord wilt thou suffer the enemy to oppress thy saints. Destruction hath come upon us like a wild wing..." Edward adds, "thou didst forewarn us...and behold, thy word is fulfilled."[20] He sought the Lord's help most earnestly but did not blame Him, even in the most dismal of times. If he seemed overly positive in his faith, one might consider historian Ranney's description of Edward and Lydia: "Without understanding the zeal to serve the Lord, you cannot understand the history of this family."[21]

During the pages ahead, we will see times when Bishop Partridge did what he thought best, but later received different instructions from the prophet. Yet, in one of the darkest periods of church history, May 2, 1833, as Jackson County mobs repelled the Missouri saints, with Edward at their immediate head, Joseph could write, "I am thankful to the Lord for the testimony of his spirit, which he has given me concerning your honesty and sincerity before him, and the Lord loveth you, and also Zion, for he chasteneth whom he loveth...In these words, Heavenly Father in the name of Jesus Christ thy son, preserve brother Edward, the bishop of thy church and give him wisdom, knowledge and power, and the Holy Ghost, that he may impart to the saints in Zion their inheritances..."[22]

Lydia labored in silent but patient support of Edward. Like many other wives of the Dispensation of the Fullness of Times, especially prior to the exodus westward, nothing is mentioned of her in the Doctrine and Covenants. There is little more in official church history. We learn much about Lydia through her diaries and letters, as well as those of her children. With Edward gone so much on church business, it was up to Lydia to set the daily example for the children, to teach them the tenets of their new religion and most probably, why not all neighbors and associates embraced those tenets as enthusiastically as did their parents.

In Painesville, Lydia's motherhood duties were directed toward five daughters, Eliza Maria, Emily Dow, Harriet Pamelia, Caroline Ely, Lydia, and and a son, Clisbee (who died in infancy). It was no little chore to remove this brood to Missouri. After moving there, she had a son they named Edward Jr. All kept Lydia quite as busy as her husband. If Edward was a man without guile, Lydia was a woman who appreciated and complemented his spiritual aims. The two would need such strengths for the challenges about to unfold before them.

end notes, chapter two

1. "Long Journal of Edward Partridge," LDS Church Archives, Salt Lake City, UT
2. Ibid
3. Ibid.
4. Ibid
5. Partridge, Scott Herald, unpublished manuscript, "Edward Partridge, the First Bishop," p. 108. On microfilm, LDS Church Archives, Req. No. 316573; call no. MS 14876.
6. Ibid, pp. 105-106
7. "The Journal of Bishop Edward Partridge, 1818," transcribed by Lyman DePlatt, p. 2.
8. It may also be simply that Edward had gained more maturity in his writing, as this journal was penned 17 years later than the first.
9. "Edward Partridge Journal, 1835" (missionary journey), p. 26
10. "Long Journal of Edward Partridge," LDS Church Archives
11. *Other Drums*, p. 115; also quoted by S. H. Partridge, p. 9. While this is fiction and does not represent documented history, it does indicate a perception of Edward's dilemma as bishop by a Partridge descendent.
12. H. S. Partridge, p. 98
13. Ibid, p. 99
14. Diaries of Emily and Eliza in their later years. See "Sources Cited" for names and access to these diaries.
15. This blessing was given Edward in 1835, indicating the type of man that Partridge might become if faithful, but more especially, the challenge he would have in his earthly ministry.
16. "Long Journal of Edward Partridge," pp. 12-13. LDS Church Archives.
17. Page 41 in today's LDS Hymnbook
18. "Long Journal of Edward Partridge," pp. 75-76. LDS Church Archives.
19. "EP Journal, 1835-36," p. 68
20. "EP Journal," LDS Church Archives.
21. Lucretia Lyman Ranney, *Our Priceless Heritage*, part II, p. 6
22. "EP Journal," LDS Church Archives

chapter three

Mormon Concept of Zion

To better understand the role of Edward Partridge in his assignment to establish Zion in Missouri, we need to better understand the concept of Zion itself. The concept as a blessing for the Lord's obedient was hinted at as early in the Old Testament as Enoch's era in Genesis 5:24. "He [Enoch] walked with God...for God took him." Blessings given the obedient Enoch are mentioned thusly in the Pearl of Great Price (available to the saints in 1830) Moses 7:13: "He [Enoch] spake the word of the Lord and the Earth trembled, and the mountains fled, even according to his command...all nations feared greatly, so great was the power of the language which God had given him." This, it should be remembered, was the same Enoch complaining to God earlier (Moses 6:31) that he was "slow of speech" and the people would not heed his word.[1]

Moses 7:19-21 adds: "And Enoch continued his preaching in righteousness unto the people of God. And it came to pass in his days, that he built a city that was called the City of Holiness, even Zion." Here, Zion is mentioned as a geographical place. In process of time Zion "was taken into Heaven." We further read that the Holy City shall be returned. "...righteousness and truth will I cause to sweep the earth as with a flood, to gather out mine elect from the four quarters of the earth, unto a place which I shall prepare, an Holy City, that my people may gird up their loins, and be looking forth for the time of my coming...and it shall be called Zion, a New Jerusalem."[2]

The saints of the latter days would naturally be looking eagerly forward to the return of Zion as mentioned in Moses 7:18: "And the Lord called his people Zion, because they were of one heart and one mind, and dwelt in righteousness; and there was no poor among them." Here was a promise to buoy up the hearts of all yearning for a closer spiritual relationship with their Father in Heaven.³

But were these references to the "Holy City" of Jesus Christ's earthly ministry in the Meridian of Times, or the latter days? Most assuredly the latter, for Moses 7:6 says... "they shall see us; and we shall fall upon their necks, and they shall fall upon our necks and we will kiss each other. And there shall be mine abode, and it shall be Zion, which shall come forth out of all the creations I have made; and for the space of a thousand years shall the earth rest."

This statement obviously represents a period just prior to ushering in of the Millennial era rather than during or immediately following the Saviour's earthly ministry. David makes it even more clear in Psalms 102:16: "When the Lord shall build up Zion, he shall appear in his glory." Clearly, the Lord did not appear in his glory when crucified in the Meridian of Times.

The return of Zion is further described in Isaiah 2:2-3 as follows: "And it shall come to pass in the last days that the mountain of the Lord's house shall be established in the top of the mountains, and shall be exalted above the hills; and all nations shall flow unto it. And many people shall go and say,' Come ye and let us go up to the mountain of the Lord, to the house of the god of Jacob;and he will teach us of his ways, and we will walk in his paths; for out of Zion shall go forth the law, and the Word of the Lord from Jerusalem.'" Isaiah 35:10 says: "And the ransomed of the Lord shall return and come to Zion with songs and everlasting joy upon their heads; they shall obtain joy and gladness, and sorrow and sighing shall flee away. And then they will be delivered from the overflowing scourge which will pass through the land." (It should be noted here for later reference that the inhabitants of Zion would first pass through a "scourge" before the Lord delivers them.) In Isaiah 51:16 the Lord adds, "And I have put my words in thy mouth...and say unto Zion, Thou art my people."

Eager to be "my people," Joseph and the saints looked forward to the Promised Land, not only as a geographical place of refuge but also an economic and spiritual "utopia" where there "will be no poor among them."⁴ So important was this concept to the latter-day saints in the Restoration that it was emphasized in the Doctrine and Covenants in sections 6, 11, 12, 14 in 1829, even before official organization of the church. The precise location was not made known at this time but the saints were admonished to "...keep my commandments and seek to bring forth and establish the cause of Zion." Thus, it was a concept well understood by faithful latter-day saints before it was a precise location.

It was a singular honor that Edward should be chosen as the one to help buy and equitably distribute lands in the new Zion "that there be no more poor among you." Note also the language recorded by Joseph in D&C 45:65-67, "And with one heart and one mind, gather up your riches that ye may purchase an inheritance which shall thereafter be appointed unto you. And it shall be called the New Jerusalem, a land of peace, a city of refuge, a place of safety for the saints of the Most High God...it shall be called Zion."

Here, indeed, was one of the final glorious promises in the "Restitution of all things."

All speculation about where the new Zion would be ended on July 20, 1831 when Joseph Smith announced this revelation given in D&C 57:1-2: "Hearken O ye elders of my church, saith the Lord your God, who have assembled yourselves together, according to my commandments, in this land, which is the land of Missouri, which is the land I have appointed and consecrated for the gathering of the saints. Wherefore, this is the land of promise, and the place for the city of Zion...Behold the place which is now called Independence is the center place." Instructions were then given to build the temple westward near the courthouse. Edward Partridge was told specifically that it was his duty to "divide unto the saints their inheritance..." And now concerning the gathering — Let the bishop [Edward] and the agent make preparations for those families which have been commanded to come to this land, as soon as possible, and plant them in their inheritance."

When it became known that the new Zion was Jackson County, Missouri, few knew much about this remote land a thousand miles from Church headquarters in Kirtland, Ohio. Initially, those who hearkened to the call and settled in Missouri found rich soil, green meadows and forests, ample rainfall and many reasons to embrace their new homes with high expectations for a happy future both for themselves and incoming brethren. LDS historian B. H. Roberts suggests that the beginning of Zion in the last days was the laying of a foundation for a log cabin in Kaw Township, Colesville Branch, just west of Independence. "...the first log was carried by 12 men, of whom the Prophet was one, in honor of the 12 tribes of Israel. Sidney Rigdon consecrated the land to the gathering of the saints..." Said Joseph Smith, "It was a season of joy and afforded a glimpse of the future which time will yet unveil to the foundation of the faithful."[5]

However, after the old settlers began to witness more and more Mormons buying land among them, they were to become apprehensive about the incoming strangers. No doubt, some of these saints traveling to Zion may have unwisely informed local inhabitants that the Lord had promised Jackson County to them. Watching the "Mormon invasion" swell, locals began to grow increasingly apprehensive. Some saints were to ask, particularly after being welcomed rather rudely, "Why Missouri?" When persecutions increased, and lives were directly threatened, other saints began to wonder openly if Joseph had truly spoken for the Lord in naming western Missouri as Zion. A few seemingly expected a refuge for all their previous troubles. As historian D. Brent Collette put it in a master's thesis study, "In 1831, anticipating and preparing for the advent of the Savior, the young enterprising Mormon Church undertook to establish a millennial utopia, known as 'Zion,' or the 'New Jerusalem,' in Jackson County, Missouri. The established Missourians, however, took violent exception to Mormon intruders, who to them represented a threat to established social, economic, political and religious conventions."[6]

The Missourians didn't trust the Mormons on several matters. The Missourians were well aware that the Latter-day Saints taught "free agency," were adamantly opposed to slavery as practiced in the South and would vote against them in any issue involving keeping of slaves. For that matter, the Missourians feared anyone and everyone advocating abolition, including those flocking to the Kansas region to the west, likely sooner or later enter the Union as anti-slave under the Missouri Compromise.

In addition, the Book of Mormon taught that the Indians or "Lamanites" were a chosen people of God as much Israelites as the Jews of the Old Testament. Missourians who had fought a number of battles with the Indians over territorial rights were determined not to relinquish their lands, and looked upon the neighboring Indians with great distrust. Now here come these Mormons claiming the Indians to be a "chosen people of God," trying to proselyte them and accord them a place in decent society.

Furthermore, western Missouri was the nation's western frontier for jumping off into the wilderness, the trailhead for Oregon and Santa Fe trails, and had until recently been a primary market for the fur trade. It was a natural gathering place for what many called "border ruffians," plus fugitives of the law resenting all government and/or unfamiliar religious restrictions. Thus, the Missourians' philosophical views were bound to come into conflict with the Mormon immigrants no matter their diligence in being righteous and circumspect.

How did Edward Partridge respond to the opposition of the old settlers in Missouri and consequent murmuring of the rebuffed saints? There is nothing to indicate other than that he stood solidly behind the prophet in attempting to facilitate the saints' gathering as commanded in the Doctrine and Covenants. He seemed to concern himself with little else but trying to establish Zion according to the Prophet's revelations. He might have questioned "Why Missouri?" but once the command came, Edward set about immediately to prove his obedience.

It is interesting, however, that Joseph himself appeared surprised on his first visit to Missouri that it had been selected as the new Zion. On his initial visit to the "Show Me State" in 1831, he records in the Documentary History of the Church, page 189, the following: "...Our reflections were many, coming as we had from a highly cultivated state of society in the east, and standing now upon the confines or western limits of the United States, and looking into the vast wilderness of those that sat in darkness; how natural it was to observe the degradation, leanness of intellect, ferocity and jealousy of a people that were nearly a century behind the times, and to feel for those who roamed about without the benefit of civilization, refinement, or religion; yea, and exclaim in the language of the Prophets, 'When will wilderness blossom as the rose? When will Zion be built up on her glory, and where will Thy temple stand, unto which all nations shall come in the last days?'"

Joseph says his anxiety and those with him were "soon relieved" in D&C Sect. 57. Jackson County was "the gathering place for the saints, the land of promise and the place for the city of

Zion...and thus saith the Lord your God, if you will receive wisdom, here is wisdom."

The ideal of economic equality, or the Law of Consecration ("let there be no poor among you") and Partridge's role in it within the new Zion is explained thusly by Collette: "...as the first bishop of the Church, he [Edward Partridge] was...the first administrator of the Zion economic system under the Prophet, Joseph Smith...within the Church, this trend of utopianism had been evident in a 'common stock,' a communitarian practice...as one of the first members of the Latter-day Saints faith, his [Edward's] life is a representation of the struggles, persecutions and sacrifices of early Mormon history."[7]

The LDS concept of consecration was not as utopian as the idealistic state described by Plato in *The Republic* among the Greeks in 300 B. C. wherein all was done in common. Mormon participants did not eat at a common table nor wear identical clothes. The Law had nothing to do with the often cruel communism practiced by Soviet regimes later in the 1900s, where all citizens yielded to government takeover, and material goods distributed without vote. Under the LDS concept of consecration, saints would agree to help the poor among them in an atmosphere of spiritual comraderie but with no fear of physical punishment. It should be added, truthfully, that social ostracism might, however, follow those unwilling to live the Law of Consecration. For those entering and demanding return of all "donations," excommunication could result. How successful the program might be, of course, depended heavily upon how fairly individual goods were disbursed. This placed a deep burden upon the shoulders of Edward Partridge as bishop to see that all were treated equitably. Since he was the first bishop, there was no precedent to follow, no one to model after. Meantime, there were many questions. Who to be precise, were the "poor"? What if they were poor because they were unwilling to work? What if they contributed nothing? What if they did not announce their coming to Zion as required?

The idea of "consecrating" oneself to the Lord is given as a commandment as early in the Bible as Exodus 28:41. The "Law of Consecration" is introduced into the New Testament in Acts 2:44: "And all that believed were together, and had all things common; and sold their possessions and goods, and parted them to all men, as every man had need." The same is mentioned in Mosiah 4:21 (some 124 years before the Book of Acts was written), "...oh how you ought to impart of the substance that ye have to one another." Later, the Law of Consecration was explained in the D&C 42:30-31 with these words: "And behold thou wilt remember the poor and consecrate of thy properties for their support that which thou hast to impart unto them, with a covenant and deed which cannot be broken...and inasmuch as ye impart of your substance unto the poor, ye will do it unto me..." Verse 32 adds that one's material goods should be placed before the bishop of the Church [Partridge] and each man shall be a steward over... that which he has received by consecration." Then followed the warning: "For if ye are not equal in earthly things ye cannot be equal in obtaining heavenly things."[8]

Thus, the Law was not just an expectation of entering into a sharing relationship of property but a duty of all those who could call themselves saints. The concept was often referred to as the United Order.[9] It was simply another name for the Law of Consecration.[10]

This Law or Order, no doubt, did not set well with the Missourians. But there was opposition to the saints well before Partridge introduced consecration to Jackson County. Joseph Smith says as early as May 1831 that the saints met opposition in missionary journeys into Missouri:[11] "The Elders now began to go to the western country, two and two, according to the word of the Lord...and as the mission to western Missouri and the gathering of the saints to that place was the most important subject which then engrossed the church, I will here insert the copy of a letter [from Oliver Cowdery] received about this time from Kaw Township, Missouri [12 miles west of Independence]: "...the letter received from you informed us that the opposition was great against you. Now, our beloved brethren, we verily believe that we also can rejoice that we are counted worthy to suffer...for His name. All the devils from the infernal pit are united and foaming out their own shame [against us]. God forbid that I should bring a railing accusation against them, for vengeance belongeth to Him who is able to repay."

Cowdery named not only atheists but many Christian churches who were united against the message of the Restoration. If the prophet did not worry himself about the stone wall Cowdery encountered, it might have been because opposition to the church was mounting everywhere. Joseph recorded that an earthquake in China, predicted by an LDS girl, was blamed on the Mormons.[12] Whether she actually caused it mattered little. If a Mormon, she was guilty.

After Edward arrived in Missouri with the prophet to begin purchasing lands, both were present for the dedicating of the Temple in the center place of Zion a little west of Independence, as outlined D&C Sect 57. When Joseph later left for Kirtland he wrote: "After ascertaining the very spot [for the temple dedication] and having the happiness of seeing quite a number of the families of my brethren comfortably situated upon the land, I took leave of them and journeyed back to Ohio, and used every influence and argument that lay in my power to get those who believed in the everlasting covenant, whose circumstances would admit...to remove to the place which I had designated to be the land of Zion." But Joseph adds that many "having a zeal not according to knowledge and not understanding the doctrine of the church have, no doubt, said many things which are derogatory to the general principles of the Church." The prophet added that apologies "would be issued if they would do any good."[13]

Smith did not elaborate on this statement, but it appears some saints settling in Zion may have said things which made it difficult for others who followed.

With the foregoing revelations placing a heavy burden upon Edward to prepare Zion for the saints' coming, he decided not to accompany other church members, including Joseph, back to Kirtland. Edward would "stand in the office," and "plant" himself in the new Zion. He would ask Lydia and the children to join him in Missouri. He emphasized that it was her decision to do so, but he could not leave his office at that time to return for her. He also warned her that the prospects for comfort in Missouri were "poor" compared to their lifestyle in Ohio, and "if she came, she would have to suffer many privations here which you and I have not been used to for years."[14]

Lydia was not the kind to shrink from duty. She would do her part that her husband might do his. She would also leave her home knowing full well she would probably never see it again. Since it was not considered safe for a woman to travel with large sums of money, she entrusted $500 to a friend. She never saw it again.[15] Then, she joined the Isaac Morley family and others in leaving Ohio in the fall of 1831. Inclement weather halted the Partridge-Morley families along banks of the Missouri River where she was fortunate to find shelter with a friendly non-member family in that region.[16] She remained until Edward arrived to bring her and the family the remainder of the way to Independence. After arriving, Lydia did, indeed, find that "Missouri was not like Ohio." Ironically, her first residence in Missouri was a log cabin rented from Lilburn W. Boggs who was to be a key figure as governor in later exterminating the Mormons from Missouri.[17]

Lydia detailed in her journal immediate differences in the people and cultures of Missouri and Ohio. The former's language and dialect included phrases like "I reckon" and "a right smart chance." Instead of carrying things in their hands, the people balanced them on their heads. Children were toted on a hip and in warm weather, women often went barefoot, children shirtless. "Everything seemed to be after the backwoods style."[18]

Historian Roberts describes the Missourians of that period thusly: "They had no disposition to beautify their homes, or even make them convenient or comfortable. They lived in their log cabins without windows and very frequently without floors other than the ground; and the dingy, smoked log walls were unadorned by pictures or other ornaments. they were uneducated; those who could read or write being the exception; and they had an utter contempt for the refinements of life...narrow-minded, ferocious, and jealous of those who sought to obtain better homes and who aspired to something better in life than had yet entered the hearts of these people."[19]

Roberts adds that the Missourians made up many accusations against the Mormons, perhaps the most serious being that they encouraged slaves to leave their masters and that "free people of color might be welcome in Jackson County." It would appear that no matter how delicately and sensitively the saints might "take up their inheritance" as part of the Law of Consecration in Jackson County, the old settlers took a dim view about having these religious zealots in their midst.

Nevertheless, Edward and Lydia stood in readiness for the faithful saints to gather and flourish on the western border of the United States as prescribed by revelation from Joseph Smith. The ranks were to swell in Missouri with these verses in D&C 62:2-6: "And verily mine eyes are upon those who have not as yet gone up unto the land of Zion; wherefore your mission is not yet full...and now continue your journey. Assemble yourselves upon the land of Zion...behold, I the Lord have brought you together that the promise might be fulfilled, that the faithful among you should be preserved and rejoice together in the land of Missouri..."

If there had been doubt about where loyal saints should gather, this revelation made it clear.[20] No doubt, Partridge resolved more diligently to be prepared. There was much work to do in purchasing lands for those coming in and deciding how they should be divided. The saints had a responsibility to bring money for purchase with them, as well as a member-in-good-standing "recommend" from their home elders.[21] It was Edward who must determine if the member "passed muster." It would be difficult for him to tell an incoming saint that, "Sorry, you'll have to go back. This isn't sufficient money for the land you'll need." In general, much federal land was available at $1.25 per acre, with most saints obtaining up to 30 acres. This was relatively little considering that the Homestead Act of 1862 was to portion out 160 acres per head of household in order to provide sustenance.[22]

As a guide, Edward received this revelation through the Prophet Joseph: "Hearken unto me, saith the Lord God, and I will speak unto my servant Edward Partridge, and give unto him directions; for it must needs be that he receive directions how to organize this people. For it must needs be that they be organized according to my laws; if otherwise, they will be cut off. Wherefore, let my servant Edward Partridge, and those whom he has chosen, in whom I am well pleased, appoint unto this people their portions, every man equal according to his family, according to his circumstances and wants and needs. And let my servant Edward Partridge, when he shall appoint each man his portion, give unto them a writing that shall secure unto his portion, that he shall hold it, even this right and this inheritance in the church, until he [general church member] transgresses and is not accounted worthy by the voice of the church according to the laws and covenants of the church."[23] The revelation then states that the member shall forfeit said property if leaving the church for any reason and the goods shall go to a church storehouse to be administered by

Edward to the poor and needy. He is then told to reserve goods as needed by the wants and needs of his own family.

Edward is given three directives in this revelation: (1) determine needs and "wants" of each family, with the former being more important than the latter; (2) determine in the absence of the prophet when a participant has "transgressed" his inheritance, (3) determine how much of the consecrated goods could be appropriated for his own family. It seems inherent in working full time for the church that Edward could be justified in taking from the donations of others for his own family. (But family members said he never did so.)[24] Clearly, both the Lord and Joseph entrusted Partridge with a difficult assignment, one that only a man "without guile" and "a pattern of piety" — and the wisdom of Solomon — might carry out.

In the months following dedication of the temple site in Jackson County, in which Edward participated,[25] Joseph instructed W.W. Phelps to take a printing press with him to Independence. The building housing the press was dedicated by Partridge. While publishing the Evening and Morning Star newspaper each month would include revelations on moving to Zion, the same might also raise the hackles of local Missourians. One such item appearing in the Star's prospectus early in 1832 stated: "…this paper is sent forth, that a wicked world may know that Jesus Christ, the Redeemer, who shall come to Zion, will soon appear."[26]

Interestingly during this time, doubters of Joseph Smith's prophetic calling, in particular new member William E. M'Lelland, attempted to produce their own "revelation" from the Lord. Joseph says that M'Lelland, "the wisest man in his own estimation, having more learning than sense, endeavored to write a commandment unto one of the least of the Lord's…and failed. It was an awful responsibility to write in the name of the Lord."[27] M'Lelland would show up later to vex the prophet in other ways.

During this young period of growth in the new church, there were often confusing directions, or at least they were perceived that way by some members. For example, was Edward Partridge always in charge of church matters in the new Zion, where some thousand saints had gathered, or were traveling apostles and counselors from Kirtland, say the Prophet's First Counselor Sidney Rigdon, in charge upon arrival? In particular, when Edward wrote to Kirtland for instructions...should those who were sent advise only...or take over? Refinements of duty had not been worked out in the fledgling church, or at least successfully sorted through and interpreted to the satisfaction of all members. At a conference held in Jackson County in 1832, housekeeping matters as needed "to organize and set order in Zion" were finally accomplished.[28] Partridge, as "housekeeper" in his own "kitchen," could breathe a little easier. The job was difficult enough without myriad points of confusion.

Just prior to the prophet's second visit to Jackson County, Joseph was tarred and feathered by an Ohio mob. Joseph recognized some of the mobbers as former members of the Campbellite church, and one Simons Ryder who had just defected from the LDS faith. Even more badly injured than Joseph was Sidney Rigdon who was dragged across the ice on his head. Rigdon went "crazy," in the prophet's words, and asked for a razor to kill both Joseph and his wife.[29] It was a difficult time for church members and no less for Edward and Lydia Partridge, for among the chaos, particularly in Missouri, someone in high authority had to maintain a calm head and keep the struggling church moving forward.[30] Many prominent church members at this time were cautioned in the Doctrine and Covenants that "Satan desired their souls" and they must guard against temptation and failure to act according to conviction. It was a time when the hearts of the weak would fail and estrange themselves from the church. It was a time of sifting to determine who had the faith to continue. In some cases, mobbers and persecutors sought in almost demon-like fury to force the saints, whether in Ohio or Missouri, to "confess" their disbelief in the Book of Mormon and Mormonism. Only if done would torture be withdrawn.

Yet, there were many moments of joy for Missouri saints of the early 1830s, especially when a strengthening member came on the scene to buoy sagging spirits. Upon arriving in Independence on his second visit, Joseph said, "We found the brethren in Zion, generally enjoying good health and faith; and they were extremely glad to welcome us among them." At a general conference of the church soon thereafter, "the right hand of fellowship was given me by the Bishop, Edward Partridge, in behalf of the church. The scene was solemn, impressive and delightful. During the intermission, a difficulty or hardness which had existed between Bishop Partridge and Elder Rigdon, was amicably settled and when we came together in the afternoon, all hearts seemed to rejoice."[31]

The prophet did not elaborate on the "hardness"[32] between Edward and Sidney, but in earlier revelations both Partridge and Rigdon had been mildly chastened by the Lord. D&C 64:16-17 says, mentioning previous deviators, "...they condemned for evil that which was not evil; nevertheless, I have forgiven my...servant Edward Partridge, behold he hath sinned and Satan seeketh to destroy his soul. But when these things are made known unto them and they repent of the evil, they shall be forgiven."

The exact circumstances were not given. It was one of the few times Edward was ever officially chastened. He may have said something about matters not going as smoothly in purchasing lands in Missouri as he had hoped. Or that members were not cooperating as Edward thought they should in living the Law of Consecration. Times were stressful enough without anyone openly voicing complaints.

The rebuke against Rigdon was more severe: "...I the Lord am not pleased with my servant Sidney Rigdon; he exalted himself in his heart, and received not counsel, but grieved the spirit. Wherefore, his writing is not acceptable unto the Lord and he shall make another; and if he receiveth it not, behold he standeth no longer in the office to which I have appointed him." A few verses later, the Lord warns, "For this is a day of warning, and not a day of many words. For I, the Lord, am not to be mocked in the last days."[33]

Sidney had been commanded to write a description of Zion under the prophet's direction and the same was declared by revelation as "unacceptable," possibly due to negative or biased comments by Rigdon. Specifics, however, are not given.

By April of 1832, relationships between saints and past settlers in Missouri became so strained that Joseph wrote: "On the 27th, we transacted considerable business for the salvation of the saints, who were settling among a ferocious set of mobbers, like lambs among wolves..." But the prophet was undaunted "...on the 28th and 29th, I visited the brethren above Big Blue River, in Kaw Township, a few miles west of Independence, and received a welcome only known by brethren and sisters united as one in the same faith, and by the same baptism and supported by the same Lord... It is good to rejoice with the people of God."[34]

From pages 316 to 375 of Joseph's Vol.1 History of the Church, letters between Kirtland and Independence reflect the great concern members felt for one another in time of trial. Storm clouds hovered over both Mormon settlements but the saints in Missouri suffered the greatest tribulations in that their lives were daily threatened. Letters from Missouri were often full of complaint that the Ohio saints had it easier. "Our hearts are greatly grieved," wrote Joseph to W. W. Phelps, "at the spirit which is breathed both in your letter and that of Brother [Sidney] Gilbert's...Tell Brother Gilbert that low insinuations God hates. But he rejoices in an honest heart...if the fountain of our tears be not dried up, we will still weep for Zion...Hear the warning voice of God, lest Zion fall, and the Lord sware in His wrath the inhabitants of Zion shall not enter into His rest...this from your brother who trembles for Zion and for the wrath of Heaven, which awaits her if she repents not."

Joseph then laments that some letters sent to Zion have not made their way to Bishop Partridge and asks all saints in Missouri, upon receipt of any letter from himself or any church official in Kirtland, to share it with the man who is in charge of church matters in Zion, Bishop Partridge. In theory then, Edward would see all such letters sent to Missouri, and ponder the "wrath of God" which beset the members there if each did not do his part. It is likely with such communication from the prophet that Edward more fully resolved to assist in "purifying" Zion and do all in his power to see that the saints were worthy of the promised blessings there.

Edward Partridge wrote no known letter of grievance during this trying time as had Phelps and Gilbert. He did, however, send a list of questions to the prophet inquiring about proper procedure in the matter of consecrating property to the church. Joseph clarified the issue by saying both member and bishop must agree on the "surplus" that the member is willing to place at Edward's disposal for the poor and needy.[35] "The matter of consecration must be done by the mutual consent of both parties." If the bishop alone decides what is right, he would "have more power than a king." If vice versa, Zion would be "thrown into confusion" and "make a slave of the bishop." Participants, says Joseph, "must reasonably show to the bishop that they need as much as they claim." If it can't be decided how much the participant should donate or how much he needs, the case must be laid before a council of 12 high priests..."

An example of a member consecrating his goods to Bishop Partridge is seen in this transaction with Titus Billings. "Be it known that I, Titus Billings of Jackson County, and the state of Missouri, having become a member of the Church of Christ...do of my own free will and accord, having first paid my just debts, grant and hereby give unto Edward Partridge...bishop of said church...the following property, viz. — sundry articles of furniture valued $55.27, also two beds...for the purpose of purchasing lands in Jackson County, Mo. and building up the New Jerusalem, even Zion, and for relieving the wants of the poor and needy. For which I, Titus Billings, do covenant and bind myself and my heirs forever."[36]

Bishop Partridge, for his part, "having received the above described property, of the said Titus Billings, do bind myself, that I will cause the same to be expended for the above mentioned purposes of the said Titus Billings to the satisfaction of the church."

Edward then signs another document leasing to Billings a parcel of land with the legal description to be recorded in church and Jackson County records. Billings pledges to pay taxes on the property and "to also pay yearly unto the said Edward Partridge, Bishop of said Church...all that I shall make or accumulate more than is needful for the support and comfort of myself and family..."This document prepared by Bishop Partridge would be binding unless "he [Titus Billings] transgresses and is not deemed worthy by the authority of the Church...to belong to the Church. And in that case, I, the said Titus Billings, do acknowledge that I forfeit all claim to the above described leased and loaned property, and hereby bind myself to give back the lease and also pay an equivalent, for the loaned articles for the benefit of said Church, unto the said Bishop Partridge, Bishop of said Church."

Note that if the participant backs out for any reason, he must pay the Church for the use of the goods and property which have been "loaned" to him.

Edward then pledges himself to provide from the storehouse for Titus Billings and his family in case of sickness, old age etc. "to administer to their necessities." From this document, we can ascertain the responsibility of Bishop Partridge in establishing the Law of Consecration in Zion for thousands of saints in addition to

Billings who would follow the Lord's directives to settle in Missouri. For every saint entering this agreement, there would also be some wanting to extricate themselves from it for various reasons; Edward would have to determine if there were any mitigating circumstances among their "necessities," entitling them to keep any of their contractual "inheritance."

Some critics of this period in LDS Church history have pointed to the "peculiarities" of the Mormons and their "all things in common" philosophies for fostering misunderstanding and distrust among the Missourians. Misunderstanding and distrust did, indeed, abound; but it seemed to have little to do with the saints adhering to the Law of Consecration. Persecution had begun well before the Church in Missouri could begin practicing the law on any wholesale scale.

History records that said persecution rapidly worsened. By early 1833, mob violence was mushrooming in Jackson County to the extent that haystacks and livestock sheds were set on fire; crops were destroyed; windows broken. Mormon homes were soon gutted by arson, threatening notes left against lives. Edward's reaction seemed to be stoic. The early Christians had been persecuted for their faith; so it would in the latter-day church. Had not Mormons been persecuted upon the first preachment of Joseph in upper New York State? The saints had come to expect it as a necessary trial of their faith, even the "buffetings of Satan"experienced by the early day saints. Yet, why should Zion, the designated "land of refuge," be so beset with hatred and violence?

There were intermittent periods of hope. Joseph himself wrote frequent, compassion-filled letters to the saints in Jackson County in an attempt to lift their spirits. Powerful sermons were preached by Rigdon to encourage the downtrodden members. Joseph wrote that in Jackson County, Sidney "preached two most powerful discourses, which so far as outward appearances was concerned, gave grave satisfaction to the people." But the fact remained that Jackson County saints saw no means by which they might assuage the wrath of the old settlers.

Much of that wrath seemed directed at the Partridge family, since Edward was known to be the man responsible for dispersion of Mormon property in the new "Zion." Members often gathered at the Partridge home "that they might be ready for any emergency." Neighboring women and children, too afraid to spend the nights in their own homes, occupied the Partridge's upstairs room. Guns were kept in readiness against mob violence; two guns, apparently being handled by those unfamiliar with firearms, discharged accidentally, sending bullets into the room above, but luckily no one was there at the time."[37]

Talk of mobs became a "perfect terror to the children." Emily Partridge, age 7, wrote that her little sister screamed out into the night with fear. But what could Edward and Lydia and the other families do more than they had done. The saints were commanded by revelation to settle in Zion. Remaining was clearly viewed as a test of their faith.

While Mormons today might wonder why the Missourians couldn't understand the saints' utmost determination to fulfill their leader's directive, how many Mormons today would look kindly upon a member of the Hare Krishna, or some other "unusual" sect declaring that their "prophet" had commanded them to amass their numbers among the saints? Looking at it this way, the "Mormon problem" must have appeared overwhelming to many Missouri Protestants.

But hadn't the Lord declared there would be "refuge" for the saints in western Missouri? It would seem more than mere speculation that Edward was puzzled. How did the Lord expect him to deal with this?

It should be realized that Joseph Smith himself seemed to struggle with the enigma. Why had the saints met such savage opposition in Jackson County, given that it was designated by the Lord himself as the "Promised Land," the Zion of the last days? Indeed, the prophet penned these words in his church history shortly after the saints were expelled from Jackson County:[38] "I cannot learn from any communication from the Spirit to me, that Zion has forfeited her claim to a celestial crown, notwithstanding the Lord has caused her to be thus afflicted, except it may be some individuals who have walked in disobedience, and forsaken the new covenant...I have always expected Zion would suffer some affliction...but I would remind you... that after much tribulation cometh the blessing...I know that Zion in the due time of the Lord will be redeemed...but how many will be the days of her purification, tribulation and affliction, the Lord has kept hid from my eyes; and when I inquire concerning this subject, the voice of the Lord is: Be still and know that I am God."

Joseph emphasized, "...there are two things of which I am ignorant; and the Lord will not show them to me, perhaps for a wise purpose in Himself... Why God has suffered so great a calamity to come upon Zion...and by what means he will return her back to her inheritance. These two things...are not plainly shown unto me."

The prophet himself sought answers. It is no wonder then that the saints who followed him, including Edward and Lydia, sought answers as well. Simply put, the saints in Missouri found themselves, as Joseph put it, in calamitous circumstances. They had made the sacrifice to be obedient and hearkened the call to come to Missouri. Now what?

end notes, chapter three

1. Moses 6:31
2. Ibid 7:62:
3. See D&C sections 43, 45
4. Moses 7:18.
5. Quoted by B. H. Roberts, *Comprehensive History of the Church* (CHC) 1:255-56.
6. "In Search of Zion: A description of early Mormon Millennial Utopianism as Revealed through the Life of Edward Partridge, master's thesis, August, 1977, Brigham Young University, Provo, UT.
7. Ibid, pp. 3,4
8. D&C 78:6
9. Attempts at living the "United Order" were made by the saints after reaching Utah, the most notable "experiment" being in Orderville, Kane County, 1875. The United Order there was disbanded within several years.
10. See D&C 104:1. As given in this verse, the concept was referred to as a "united order," (no capitalization) and later officially referred to as "The United Order."
11. Joseph Smith, *Documentary History of Church*, 1:182.
12. Ibid, 1:158. See also footnote by B. H. Roberts
13. Joseph Fielding Smith, *Teachings of the Prophet Joseph Smith*, p. 80.
14. Historian Dean Jesse, "Steadfastness and Patient Endurance: the Legacy of Edward Partridge," p. 5.
15. Lydia's comments are in the unpublished "Long Journal of Edward Partridge," LDS Church Archives, Salt Lake City, UT.
16. Ibid. Lydia said a black family "was very kind" to her and the children.
17. Jessee, p.5. "The first residence in Independence was a 'log room' rented from Lilburn W. Boggs, who later became a key figure in the expulsion of the saints from Missouri."
18. "Long Journal of Edward Partridge," LDS Church Archives, Salt Lake City, UT.
19. Roberts, p. 321. Roberts apparently gives this as his own educated opinion, minus any footnotes.
20. Many saints, including Joseph, continued to live in Kirtland. Joseph had cautioned against moving all the saints to Missouri too rapidly. As proof that members could remain in good standing while yet living in Kirtland at this time was the fact a temple was soon to be constructed there.

21. These were the forerunners of today's "temple recommends" required before faithful church members can enter the temple. During Edward's time they were to be signed by three elders of the member's local church, if the bishop or the prophet were not present.
22. Of course, more westerly lands might be less fertile than those of Missouri if less water was available. More land might well be needed farther west.
23. D&C 51:1-4. See also 5-20.
24. Edward Partridge Family Bulletin, August, 1954
25. The commandment to purchase a site for "the temple in Zion" was the direct responsibility of Bishop Partridge. He purchased 63.4 acres of land, which included the temple site, in 1831 for $130 from one Jones H. Flourney. Source: *Old Mormon Kirtland and Missouri*, Richard Holzapfel and T. Jeffery Cottle, pp. 196-99. LDS Church historian Andrew Jenson, who checked records in Independence in 1888, said city records still showed Edward Partridge as original purchaser of the temple lot site. *The Historical Record* 7:647.
26. DHC 1:259
27. DHC 1:226
28. Roberts, 1:320
29. DHC 1:265
30. It should not be supposed by this remark that others didn't stand behind Edward in his duties. While W. W. Phelps was occasionally chastened for his "complaints" in Missouri, he also wrote many eloquent letters to the governor and state officials seeking redress. Others, including Parley P. Pratt, were also present from time to time to help buoy Partridge's spirits in his difficult challenge as bishop.
31. DHC 1:267. There would, however, yet be times when Rigdon and Partridge did not agree on all matters pertaining to management of church affairs in Missouri.
32. While no specific differences were listed by Joseph, it appeared that Sidney felt Edward took on more responsibility than the prophet had given him; there is also the possibility that Rigdon was jealous of Edward's ever-growing alliance of trust with the prophet.
33. D&C 63:55-56, 58.
34. DHC 1:269
35. DHC 1:364-65.
36. The "Titus Billings contract papers" were found among records and effects of Bishop Partridge after his death, according to LDS historian B. H. Roberts, DHC 1:365-367, end notes.
37. Jesse, Dean, "Steadfast and Patient Endurance: the Legacy of Edward Partridge," p. 6
38. DHC 1:453-4. Date: Dec. 10, 1833. This letter from Joseph was written from Kirtland following reports received from W. W. Phelps and Bishop Partridge as to just how dire the saints' plight was in Missouri.

chapter four

Firestorm

The mob gave no warning. Edward turned his attention away from Lydia and newborn son Edward Jr. into a billowing ocean of waving arms and angry faces. The latter contorted into triumphant screams: "We've got him! We've got Partridge!"[1]

Edward was, indeed, a prize for the mob in its Satanic fury. He was for mobbers the chief Mormon in Missouri, responsible for dividing up their lands to the people who called themselves saints. Yet, he must have been easy prey. Edward had told his wife for weeks that he would not run from mobbers as had some of his peers. He had nothing to hide and nothing to be ashamed of.

The mob dragged Edward to the public square of Independence. Looking up, he could see only hundreds of blackened and hostile men. They gave him an ultimatum: renounce the Book of Mormon and leave the county, or suffer serious injury at their hands, perhaps death. The mob was insistent. Edward recorded his answer: "I was willing to suffer for the sake of Christ, but to leave the county, I was not then willing."[2]

"Amid an uproar of insulting shouts," the mob stripped him to his underwear and covered him with tar and feathers "from the crown of my head to my feet." It should be added that the tar of those days was more than ceremonious abuse. It was laced with acid and burned horribly. But wrote Partridge, "I bore my abuse with so much resignation and meekness that it appeared to astound the multitude, who permitted me to retire in silence, many looking very solemn, their sympathies having been touched…as to myself, I was so filled with the Spirit and love of God, that I had no hatred toward my persecutors or anyone else."[3]

One might deeply consider the magnitude of that statement.

Mind, spirit, and soul transcended physical pain. If there was any ignominy in it, the same belonged to the perpetrators. In this instance, Edward personified the meekness of Jesus Christ as he stood in spiritual power before Pontius Pilate. If the meek would, indeed, some day inherit the Earth, then Edward, herein got a start on his Celestial reward.[4] He held no animosity toward his beast-like captors, seemingly repeating in his mind Christ's statement on the cross to his Father: "Blame them not, for they know not what they do." Forgive his tormentors in their spiritual depravity, Edward did; but he would not cross Christian principles to obey their demands. Ironically, a number were Christian ministers and ecclesiastical leaders.

For seven-year old Emily Partridge, however the sight of her father returning tarred and feathered constituted a terrible memory. Emily later said she did not even recognize her father. Her sister, six-year old Caroline, says she did not recognize her father when he returned. "I thought he was an Indian and hid under the bed."[5] Later, she would write:

> My father became the first bishop of the church. He was well off until he became a Mormon, then he was driven from place to place and persecuted. We lived in one poor house after another as we moved about. In July, 1833, a number of armed men entered our home and took my father away.

Edward Sr. never afterward appeared to have the same physical vigor and vitality as before, according to family members.

The date of outrage, July 20, 1833, was one to be remembered in Latter-day Saint history, as were the tarring and feathering of Joseph Smith and Sidney Rigdon on March 24, 1832. But the events of that July evening were more sinister in that they were but a herald of persecution to be suffered by members of the Church of Jesus Christ of Latter-day Saints in Missouri. None bore a greater brunt of the Jackson County wrath in 1833 than Bishop Edward Partridge.

Joseph Smith explained the tarring and feathering incident this way:

> When Bishop Partridge, who was without guile, and Elder Charles Allen, walked off, coated like some unnamed, unknown

biped, one of the sisters cried, 'While you who have done this wicked deed, must suffer the vengeance of God, they, having endured persecution, can rejoice, for henceforth is laid up for them a crown eternal in the Heavens.'"[6] Joseph added "...while they [the persecuted saints]mourned over fallen man, they rejoiced with joy unspeakable that they were accounted worthy to suffer in the glorious cause of their Divine Master."

Joseph's history continues:

Early in the morning of the 23rd of July, the mob again assembled, armed with weapons of war..." The saints entered in an agreement with the mobbers to remove from the county with these written words: "It is understood that Oliver Cowdery, W. W. Phelps, William M'Lellin, Edward Partridge, Lyman Wight, Simeon Carter, Peter and John Whitmer and Harvey Whitlock shall remove with their families from this county on or before the first day of January next...and use their influence to induce all the brethren now here to remove as soon as possible."[7]

The mob promised no more violence if those named would affix their names to the above document. Knowing other saints prepared to move into Jackson County, the brethren named, including Partridge, offered themselves up as a ransom if other church members would be allowed to remain without being molested; but the mobbers would not accept this offer of sacrifice. They wanted all the Mormons out.[8]

Nor did they live up to their agreement in letting the Mormons move in a civilized fashion. It was not long before the mob, led by one Richard Simpson, Chairman, a colonel in the local miltia, issued a manifesto ordering the Mormons out immediately:

At a meeting called by the citizens of Jackson County, Missouri, called for the purpose of adopting measures to rid themselves of the sect of fanatics called Mormons, held at Independence on the 20th day of July, 1833...[we] deem it proper to lay before the public an expose of our peculiar situation in regard to this singular sect of pretended Christians; and a solemn declaration of our unalterable determination to amend it."[9]

The document also stated that the Mormon's *Star* printing office "was razed to the ground... [but] without bloodshed." This boastful statement "without bloodshed" bore the seal of hypocracy; for while W. W. Phelps and his family were not initially harmed as the mob destroyed the saints' printing press, it made little difference. A bloodbath soon followed.

Showing their own fanatic zeal to rid themselves of what they called "fanatic" Mormons, the mobbers pledged to each other "their lives, bodily powers, fortunes and sacred honor," to "remove the Church from Jackson County."

One paragraph in the manifesto admits that the Mormons committed no infractions of law; yet the Missourians skirt it: "The evil is one that no one could have foreseen, and is therefore, unprovided for by the laws; and the delays incident to legislation would put the mischief beyond remedy." One line says, "our lands are to be taken by the sword."[10] Also: "Of their pretended revelations from heaven — their personal intercourse with God and His angels — the maladies they pretend to heal by the laying on of hands — and the contemplated gibberage with which they habitually profane the sabbath, we have nothing to say; vengeance belongs to God alone." But history records that the mobbers left nothing to God alone. They were soon busy taking care of it themselves.

One statement sarcastically announces:

> ...we do most solemnly declare that no Mormon in the future shall move and settle in this county...that those who fail to comply with these requisitions be referred to those of their brethren who have the gifts of divination and unknown tongues to inform them of the lot that awaits them."[11]

While many reasons have been given for the persecution of the saints in Jackson County, the tone of the language indicates, most of all, religious intolerance — ironically, among a people who themselves claimed to be Christians.

The mobbers did not wait long to violate terms of the agreement forced upon the saints. By autumn, a firestorm of attack and abuse began. Even if one felt protected by a divine inner strength, one never knew what mobs were going to do next to loved ones. By October of 1833 all of the Mormons were driven from their homes. Forced into the cold, most of the saints sought exile in neighboring Clay, Ray, Van Buren, or other counties. However desirous Edward and his family might be to return home and fulfill the decree that Jackson County be Zion, neither he nor any of the saints dared recross the border. By now it was clear that the enemy was not a few malcontents but many influential holders of city and county office, magistrates, justices of the peace, the ruling class, office-holders, clergymen.[12]

Lilburn Boggs, a resident of Jackson County, showed his cynical outlook by viewing the wreckage at the printing office and home of W.W. Phelps, and saying: "You now know what our Jackson County boys can do."[13] Boggs, who was to become an open enemy of the Mormons, was at that time little known even to many Missourians. According to historian Pearl Wilcox, Boggs was a merchant for, among other things, patent medicines, advertising that his wares were "unequaled in powers in eliminating from the human system all the poisonous juices" and good for "scrofula, white swelling, rheumatism and liver complaints."[14] Boggs, apparently a "popular citizen" locally, was soon appointed first clerk of Jackson County. The saints later learned that he not only followed many actions of his peers, but spurred them into their most egregious assaults against the Mormons.

Writing on or about this period in October, 1833, Emily Partridge penned in her unpublished journal the following eloquent description of Missouri atrocities:

> ...women and children sallied forth from their gloomy retreat to contemplate with heart-wrenching anguish the ravages of a ruthless mob, in the mangled bodies of their husbands and in the destruction of their houses..."[15] Other phrases in Emily's meticulous hand-written journals include the following: "...unprotected by the arm of the law...dreary month of November staring us in the face...the mob quit whipping and began beating with clubs...continued threats of the mob that they would drive out every Mormon from the country...[Note: Emily uses the word *country* here, not Jackson County

alone]...an anguish of heart indescribable...

Later, Emily singled out among militia members one Capt. Atchison who dared buck his peers and performed with "gallantry" in trying to help the saints. Gen. Alexander Doniphan also addressed a meeting in which he said he thought the Mormons "are better citizens than many of the old settlers of Jackson County."[16] He admired the Mormons for trying to protect their fellow church members. Gen. Doniphan expressed the opinion that "unless the saints were cowards," they should be allowed to keep their arms to protect themselves. "Greater love can no man show than he who lays down his life for his brethren."

But the dissension of these two prominent Missourians was too little against too many.

In harassing the new religious group among them, the Missourians went against their own Constitution written when the state entered the Union in 1820. The same is found even now in the State Capitol Building in Jefferson City: Article XIII, Sec. 4:

> That all men have a natural and indefensible right to worship Almighty God according to the dictates of their own conscience... that no human authority can control or interfere with the rights of conscience; that no person can ever be hurt, molested, or restrained in his religious profession or sentiments if he do not disturb others in their religious worship.

It might be expected that citizens would get out of line occasionally and violate such laws. It is another matter entirely when civil administrators abdicate their responsibility to enforce those laws in wholesale fashion. Elected officials in Missouri did make one half-hearted attempt to have the militia escort Mormons seeking legal redress to the courtroom; but the militia vanished after receiving word of mob action awaiting them in Independence. Bishop Partridge was there as one subpoenaed to testify after John Ayland, district circuit judge, wrote: "It is a disgrace to the state for such acts to happen within its limits and the disgrace will attach to our official character if we neglect to take proper means to ensure the punishment due such offenders."[17] But Edward was never allowed to testify. The militia, court and state attorneys decided to ignore the judge's assessment and ordered the Mormons out of the county anyway.

To be sure, Gov. Daniel Dunklin had in writing emphasized that "the rights of all citizens were endangered if one religious group, no matter who it might be...were violated." But when it counted, he could not muster sufficient courage to go against the mob. Furthermore, he wrote,"Even if we returned you to your homes...we couldn't promise there would be no further attacks." This appeared to be true. It was also a tragic summation of the anarchy Dunklin allowed within his administration.

All of this, of course, had a particularly unsettling effect on Bishop Partridge. He was supposed to be the saints' leader in establishing Zion in Jackson County. He was charged with fulfilling a commandment from the Lord to do so. In the trying period from July to November 1833, Edward signed his name to many documents intended to bring peace. Hopes would soar with each new attempt at rationale and reason; but they would be dashed before the ink was barely dry.

In one instance, the Jackson County residents, apparently feeling guilty at what they had done, offered payment on the saints' vacated property — independent arbiters were appointed to determine the value of each saint's holdings. But the catch was that the Mormons must promise to never return to Jackson County. Being designated as Zion, of course, the saints could not make such a promise. Edward would be at the forefront in refusing to agree to such terms.

Likewise, an order from the governor for military leaders to return arms taken from the saints prior to their flight from Jackson County never materialized. This order resulted from a letter signed by Bishop Partridge and other saints; but the final result was simply one more elevated hope soon to be quashed. Edward, as bishop, presided over several meetings attempting to repatriate the saints to their rightful homes, but all negotiations with the enemy broke down. Trust itself broke down. Whatever might be promised verbally, returning to their old homes seemed certain suicide.

Joseph himself wrote to Bishop Partridge in December, 1833 saying he was confused about the realities of duress in Jackson

County. The prophet pointed out that Brother Phelps said one thing, Orson Hyde another, Phelp's account being much more serious. Joseph asked for a "correct statement of fact."[18] Joseph assures the saints in Missouri that he and others in Kirtland have no monetary means of helping them, as "we are deeply in debt and know of no means to extricate ourselves." Then this advice on fighting back: "...you should [if possessing arms] maintain your ground as long as there is a man left, as the ground upon which are you located is the place appointed of the Lord for your inheritance, and it is right in the sight of God that you contend for it to the last."[19]

Clearly, Bishop Partridge was supposed to be the spiritual leader in Missouri...and the only immediate hope of effecting economic salvation, since the Kirtland saints "had no means." But this last letter (not a revelation but "according to wisdom") seemed to place Edward in the position of *military leader*. Lyman Wight, maybe. But Edward...no. Did Christ wield a spear against the Romans and shout orders to an army of men? No. Yet, Christ did vent his anger at the money-changers in the temple who desecrated his holy edifice...physically ousting them.

Edward must have wondered what the Prophet Joseph, yea, even the Lord... expected of him in saving Zion. Had he, Edward, not been a forceful leader in all ecclesiastical matters? He had done his part in dedicating this part of the Lord's vineyard to make it a place of refuge; he had been the prophet's right hand man in purchasing the land and dedicating the temple to be built in Jackson County;[20] He had withstood mobs almost daily in Christ's name. Jesus had not lacked courage to fight. Nor had Edward lacked that courage. But, he, Edward, a military leader...fighting to the death...? Was that the Christian thing?

He would do whatever the Lord expected of him. D&C 41:9-10 told him that he "was to do all things appointed to him." Very early he had been told that if he did not carry out the Lord's work as bishop, another would be appointed in his stead.[21] He had written his wife that "I must not fail."

But how to do it? There was that direct injunction given from the Lord in October (1833) saying, "...ye shall declare whatsoever thing ye declare in my name...in the spirit of meekness." Should the saints thus lean on their own understanding in military prowess, or in meekness depend on their faith in the Lord to deliver them? Should he have fought back against the mob which tarred and feathered him? Or submitted meekly as Christ did before Pilate?

The later revelation forthcoming in D&C 105:13-14, "...I do not require at their hands to fight the battles of Zion...I will fight the battles,"[22] must have come as a direct answer to prayer for a confused Edward.

Edward also realized he must draw the line between naive belief and realistic trust. In order to carry out the Lord's work in Missouri, he had left his property in Painesville to a friend he thought he could trust, Later, Edward learned the "friend" betrayed him. He would not now have the money needed to establish his family as planned in Jackson County.[23]

In many ways, the Latter-day saints were in a lose-lose situation. (1) If they turned the other cheek, they were easy prey; no one need fear reprisal from them. The mobbers would have complete physical advantage. Already, many of the Missourians had learned that while not complete pacifists (as say, the Society of Friend, "Quakers"),[24] the Mormons would not counterattack, or attempt to ambush their foe, giving free rein for oppressors to strike first. (2) If they did fight back, it was an indication of "Mormon aggression."

In time, the bishop and other church members decided to send P. P. Pratt and W. W. Phelps to Kirtland to personally talk with the Prophet Joseph.

Did Joseph fully understand the daily plight of the saints in Missouri? Did the saints in Kirtland know how outnumbered the latter were against the enemy?

Pratt and Wight rode in the cold of winter, very poorly clad against the elements, to reach the prophet in Kirtland. They likely hoped Joseph could ride back to Missouri with them and see for himself the predicament they were in. After talking with these two brethren, Joseph seemed to better understand and sympathize with their problem; but there were difficult challenges in Ohio, too. Mob action was growing against the saints there. Partridge and the others would have to cope with their problem as best they could, prayerfully of course, but for now without the prophet's physical presence.

For many, including Edward, the problem was, could Zion (Jackson County) be vacated in good conscience? Some might accept the concept that Zion was everywhere, as said at times, "America is Zion; Zion is wherever the pure in heart are found?"[25] But one statement in Joseph's History of the Church makes it clear that Jackson County, Missouri was specifically and irrevocably designated as Zion.[26] The reasoning is this: Edward was acknowledged to be "the head of the church in Zion." Since he was not "head" anywhere but in Missouri, the statement by Joseph had to mean that Zion was in Missouri.

Besides, the Missouri saints received word in D&C 101:17-21 (Dec. 16, 1833) that Zion had not been moved: "Zion shall not be moved...notwithstanding her children are scattered...there is none other place than that which I have appointed...for the work of the gathering of my saints...until the day cometh when there is found no more room for them." Verse 71 specifically confirms that Zion is Jackson County and all lands possible should be purchased there."

In being persecuted, the Missouri saints were not without blame. Recorded in D&C 101:1-5 is the following chastening:

> "Verily, I say unto you [Joseph Smith] concerning your brethren who have been afflicted and persecuted, and cast out from the land of their inheritance — I, the Lord, have suffered the affliction to come upon them...in consequence of their transgressions. Yet I will own them...therefore, they must be chastened and tried, even as Abraham, who was commanded to offer up his only son. For all those who will not endure chastening but deny me, cannot be sanctified." The Lord then says that the saints, by their contentions, had "polluted their inheritance...they were slow to hearken unto the Lord their God; therefore, the Lord is slow to hearken unto their prayers...they esteemed lightly my counsel but in the day of their trouble, they of necessity feel after me..." Yet, the Lord will "remember mercy."[27]

Life in Zion had appeared promising in the first two years of settlement. As a missionary, Parley P. Pratt found converts here among the Missouri settlers.[28] He wrote that at first the Jackson saints "had no debts among them, no thieves, few idlers, and all seemed to worship God with one heart and one purpose..." They were a "happy people."[29] Later some of the saints were "guilty of ignoring the revelations" given in what was then called the Book of Commandments (Doctrine and Covenants today) "preaching false doctrine, fault-finding and bickering, and not living the Law of Consecration."

While acknowledging that the saints brought some misery on themselves, LDS historian B. H. Roberts emphasizes that the saints were not guilty of breaking any of man's laws, county, state or national He says, "That certain over-zealous church members may have said the Lord would give them the land of Missouri for their inheritance is doubtless true; but that they were to obtain it in any other than a legal way never entered their minds. They had been commanded of the Lord to purchase the land for an inheritance." Roberts said he examined all of the charges of the Missourians against the saints, bringing in slaves, abusing property rights etc. and could find none substantiated. He allows that the saints were guilty, however, of two things their enemies accused them of (1) embracing a peculiar religion, and (2) in some cases, of being poor. Neither, he avows, would contradict the tenets of Christ's primitive church.[30]

Mobbers seemed especially incensed that the saints claimed to have latter-day revelation. How the saints might have avoided the mob's wrath in this regard can only be left to conjecture, for it was a measure of a man's faith in the church then and now to openly believe in the same.

As for the saints being "poor," it is a strange accusation. Mobbers took over most material possessions of the saints after the exiles fled into the night with only the clothes on their backs and whatever they could carry in their hands.

In trying to live up to the Law of Consecration, church members were novices at the practice. A few members of Rigdon's flock had practiced the law under Sidney's leadership, as had a few saints at Thompson, Ohio; but attempts to administer the law wholesale fashion in Missouri ran into trouble almost from the beginning. Many saints did not forward news of their coming, nor bring sufficient funds to purchase an "inheritance" as outlined by the Prophet Joseph.[31] He had said concerning large numbers of saints migrating, "...it would be pleasing to church or churches going to Zion...[that they] should be organized and a suitable person appointed who is well acquainted with the condition of the church...and he be sent to Kirtland to inform the Bishop and procure a license from him agreeable to the revelation: by so doing, you will prevent confusion and disorder."

It is clear that there was to be coordination in relocating from Ohio to Missouri and that all possible must be done to avoid disorder and confusion. A saint wasn't to just show up and present himself to Bishop Partridge for an "inheritance." History records that some members selfishly or carelessly skirted the spirit of this law.[32]

Was failure of the saints to live the Law of Consecration the fault of Bishop Partridge? Not according to Wilford Woodruff. The latter, who would later become president of the church, records in his journal that he joined the United Order in Missouri, giving all he had to the law.[33] Woodruff said of Edward, "Bishop Partridge was one of the wisest and best men of the last generation. Like Nathanael of old, in him there was no guile. He had passed through much persecution with the Saints, for the word of God and the testimony of Jesus."[34]

In fact, in all of revelation and church history, not a word of complaint can be found by any member that Edward failed in his trusted calling as administrator of the Law of Consecration. History records it did not succeed in Zion but, of course, the saints were allowed little peace to see if the "experiment" might work. Even at this writing some 170 years later, the "Order" is not being followed anywhere among nearly 10 million church members. The masterful and influential leader Brigham Young could not force it upon his constituents, nor for that matter, could the name of deity. Such a law clearly depends upon free agency yielding to love and a spirit of unselfishness.

There seemed to be little understanding or sympathy among the watching Missourians, although many were announced Christians, regarding the incoming saints' attempt to live the Biblical principle of consecration. Many Protestant churches had established in the county by the late 1820s; ministers appeared to enjoy high social standing among their flocks. One Rev. Joab

Powell, a "pioneer Baptist preacher, traveled over the country preaching in homes and conducting camp meetings...His simple, unassuming manner won the confidence of all he met. This God-fearing preacher could hardly read or write."[35] That many ministers were openly leaders in the persecution against Mormons is something that devout Latter-day Saints like Bishop Partridge undoubtedly found difficult to either accept or comprehend.[36]

But let us digress here long enough to determine how Missouri has treated this episode in its own history. How did they portray this period of travail for the Latter-day Saints? Some historians simply pretended it didn't exist. For others, it was a mere blink on the Missouri mindset. For example, in her *Jackson County Pioneers*, author Pearl Wilcox provides minute details of Jackson County from the Louisiana Purchase to the county's birthday on Feb. 16, 1825 to 1850, without once ever once mentioning the word "Mormon!" She tells us the county was named after President Andrew Jackson, a man "greatly admired" in western Missouri because he was a military hero in the battle against the British in the Battle of New Orleans in 1815. She says, "With a force of comparatively untrained men, Gen. Jackson killed nearly 300 Britishers with only 13 Americans slain."[37]

Nothing is said about how Independence got its name, but it would not seem too great a speculation to say it came from the Declaration of Independence in which are contained the words freedom of worship. All the more galling to men like Bishop Partridge.

In his monumental 832-page *History of Jackson County, Mo.* (not counting a lengthy index) historian W. Z. Hickman provides a total of three pages about the Latter-day Saints. Labeled "The Mormons in Jackson County," it is written by LDS historian Orson F. Whitney, pages 191-94. Following that are five pages written by Walter W. Smith of the Reorganized Church of Jesus Christ of Latter-day Saints which has this one sentence about Bishop Edward Partridge:

> "[He] was the first minister of this congregation [in Independence, Mo.]." The text adds, "During the fall of 1832 there began to be friction between the new settlers and the old inhabitants...At this time there were 10 [Mormon] churches in the county with an aggregate of 1,200 members.

It appears on the surface that Hickman intended to be fair to the Mormons and all parties involved by having a Mormon write his own peoples' history (albeit rather short), the same being true for the RLDS point of view. But the histories of Hickman and Wilcox blithely tell how diligently the old settlers worked to build up the county and make it prosperous; how gallant and brave western Missourians were in patriotically responding to their nation's call to fight in the Mexican War.[38] From the point of view of Wilcox, "Jackson County became the home of a great many strong and able people, both by selection and by birth...Every visitor was welcome to partake of the simple food, whether it be a weary traveler, an agent for ague pills, a pelt hunter, or a circuit-rider preacher. The latchstring was always out."[39]

Apparently for everyone but Mormons.

Ironically, Hickman includes these lines of poetry from Jackson County, the Pride: "She is the pride, Missouri's fairest daughter...Open stands the door for all who enter..."[40]

Hickman's history also tells of the "Constitution" or rules of the Six-mile Baptist Church, prominent in Jackson County of 1825, as follows:

> (1) We believe in one only true and living god, a trinity of persons... (2) We believe that the scriptures of the old and new Testament are the word of God and the only rule of faith and practice. (3) We believe in the fall of Adam and that all his posterity fell in him and were made sinners. We believe in the corruption of human nature and the impotency of man to recover himself by his own free will or ability.[41]

The other nine could be cited (see Appendix) but in these three Baptist "Articles of faith" alone, the Latter-day saint sees multiple causes of conflict. While both churches called themselves Christians, the two scarcely held any beliefs in common. One could, perhaps, argue for baptism by immersion and that no menial work be done on the Sabbath. The Six-mile Church also made it a rule of "Decorum" that all religious meetings be opened and closed with prayer. Interestingly, the fifth "article" refers to members of Christ's church as "saints." Apparently these Baptists found nothing presumptuous with the incoming Mormons calling themselves "saints," a designation to simply mean all members, not honored mortals as defined in Catholic protocol.

There is nothing in the 12 "articles" referring in any way to "Zion." It is easy to see why the LDS concept of Zion would be foreign to the Jackson County settlers and why it might cause them to ask, "Zion...why make it Jackson County? Why bother us? We were here first...etc."

No doubt Edward suffered much during this time in seeing the high standards he espoused for Christian conduct being trampled. Many skeptics of Edward's new religion might take turns saying, "I told you so." But Edward himself saw it differently, even in 1833 at height of the Missouri persecutions. He writes:

> Since I have torn my affections from this world's goods, from the vanities and toys of time and sense, and been willing to love and serve God with all my heart, and be led by the Holy Spirit, my mind has been as it were continually expanding — receiving the things of God, until glories indescribable present themselves before me, and I am frequently led to exclaim in my own mind, why is it that men, rational men, will suffer themselves to be led in darkness down to the gulf of despair by the enemy of all righteousness, while such glories lamp up the pathway of the saints?[42]

Looking at the Mormons' Missouri miseries many years later, a student of LDS history might overtly conclude that there was no joy for the saints in the newly designated Zion. Edward's statement above seems to refute that idea, for while history records the physical outrages which took place, including the tarring and feathering of Bishop Partridge, a scrutiny of the foregoing would seem to indicate that Edward was truly buoyed by a spirit seemingly transcending human understanding.

This is not offered as speculation but an attempt at objective appraisal of Edward's writings about his own feelings. Somewhat startling they may be, considering the tragic challenge he and his family faced; but to know Edward and his spiritual strength, 150 years later, those expressed feelings must be honestly analyzed. He and his family appear to have been buoyed through the troubles they encountered in a way not fully comprehended by a later generation. Many sacrifices were obviously made for the Restored Gospel; but to know if the rewards were worth it to Edward, we would need to know more precisely what took place in his mind and soul. We can only take him at his word that "glories indescribable presented themselves before me." At the same time, it may have been an understanding or insight not fully shared at that time by his young offspring. Without their parent's greater years of experience, the period must have loomed "gloomy" indeed, as Emily penned it, during the Jackson County era.

Analogies of Edward's Christ-like calm through this holocaust of wrath and hate is often spoken of in LDS philosophy as "going through the refiner's fire." The latter is described by the *World Book Encyclopedia* as a term for "the processes which remove impurities from impure or crude materials."[43] Heat, of course, is used to remove those impurities and while the material (or in this case, human being) goes through a terrible ordeal, the gold or silver (or individual) emerges polished and pure, of far greater worth than before.

The Partridges and saints in Jackson County were, indeed, being put through the "refiner's fire." It appears that Edward was well aware of the scriptural references to that phrase and determined to pass whatever test was required of him. Old Testament prophet Malachi had explained that test with these words:

> But who may abide the day of his (Christ) coming? And who shall stand when he appeareth? for he is like a refiner's fire... and he shall sit as a refiner and purifier of silver, that they may offer unto the Lord an offering in righteousness..."[44]

Joseph Smith said it this way in a letter to the saints: "Behold the great day of the Lord is at hand; and who can abide the day of his coming, and who can stand when he appeareth? For he is like refiner's fire...and he shall purify the sons of Levi, and purge them as gold and silver...therefore, as a church and as a people and as Latter-day Saints, offer unto the Lord an offering in righteousness..."[45]

After the saints seemed forever hopelessly driven from

Jackson County, Joseph announced in early February, 1834, a revelation to "redeem" Zion. The saints would converge on Missouri and try to wrest Zion from mob control. Undoubtedly, Joseph hoped that he could now take Gov. Dunklin at his word to reinstate the saints in their homes if they so chose. Marching to Zion ought to do away with the last doubt.

As a number of LDS histories record, the effort was not successful, at least not physically nor militarily. The effort was termed a tragic failure by anti-Mormons and even many saints who saw nothing but a 2,000-mile round trip march to the "Promised Land" with no reclamation of lost property whatsoever. Some saints, however, point to "spiritual" victories.

The LDS publication, *Our Heritage, a Brief History of the Church of Jesus Christ of Latter-day Saints*, says on p. 27 that "Zion's Camp in Missouri was organized to help the saints in Missouri who were being severely persecuted because of their religious beliefs. Many had been driven from their homes. On Feb. 24, 1834, the Lord revealed to Joseph Smith that he should organize a group of men to march to Missouri and and help restore the saints to their lands as explained in D&C 103:36. The Lord promised that his presence would go with them and that all victory and glory would be brought to pass through their diligence, faithfulness, and prayers of faith."

A total 207 men, 11 women and 11 children made the thousand-mile trek from Ohio to Missouri, according to records. The entourage, poor in monetary means if not spirit, suffered many deprivations and hardships. *Our Heritage* says that Gov. Daniel Dunklin did not keep his promise to help reinstate church members to their homes and the saints found no sympathy from the Missouri mobs who had driven them out. "Disappointed and angry, some [church members] rebelled."

The last hope seemed dashed when it became clear (1) that Dunklin's promised state militia had disappeared for good; in fact, if not wholly corrupt, Dunklin lacked sufficient backbone to keep promises to the exiled saints; (2) the saints were totally outnumbered by mobbers and militia who joined them even if Dunklin tried to keep his word; (3) no miracles had taken shape on the horizon for the saints' behalf, at least none sufficient to quell anti-Mormons' malevolence. No plagues against the enemy, no parting of the sea as in the Children of Israel's quest for their Promised Land.

There were statements from some saints, including Edward (see his prayer in Appendix) that the Lord slowed Missouri mobs at times with inclement weather. A number of mobbers chasing Mormon leaders also drowned in a skiff on the Missouri River. But if miracles in the saints' behalf, they were not sufficient to keep the attackers' armed might at bay. The saints did not find themselves in re-possession of their Jackson County homes.

Thus, did Zions Camp fail?

Joseph says no. "God was with us, and His angels went before us, and the faith of our little band was unwavering. We know that angels were our companions, for we saw them..." Was Joseph somewhat biased in this assessment, inasmuch as he organized the Camp in the first place?

Wilford Woodruff, a convert who was 14 years old at that time, recorded this in his diary as published by the *Deseret News*, Dec. 22, 1869. "We gained an experience that we never could have gained in any other way. We had the privilege of beholding the face of the prophet, and we had the privilege of traveling a thousand miles with him, and seeing the workings of the spirit of God with him, and the revelations of Jesus Christ unto him and the fulfillment of those revelations."

Brigham Young, in answer to a skeptic asking what had been accomplished with Zions Camp, answered, "All we went for. I would not exchange the experience I gained in that expedition for all the wealth of Geauga County [the location of Kirtland]."[46] Joseph undoubtedly learned the character of many saints as they made this difficult journey, for it seems there is nothing like discomfort and adversity to bring out the best and worst in men. Shortly afterward, Joseph chose the Twelve Apostles, from those deemed faithful during the Zions March, to work with him in ushering forward the Dispensation of the Fullness of Times.

Conclusion: whether you got something out of Zion's Camp depended on what you were looking for.

More difficult were the revelations recorded in the D&C which depict Zion in Jackson County as a "land of peace, a city of refuge, a place of safety for the saints of the Most High God."[47] Such statements are repeated several times in the D&C. Says historian Richard S. Van Wagoner, after repeating the above, "That did not happen."[48]

Edward and the Missouri saints were told that Zion should be redeemed in a "little season."[49] They waited, prayed and worked for it through remainder of the Missouri period. They waited in vain, for even the most faithful would agree that the concept of Zion as a "place of refuge" in Missouri has not yet taken place.

How long a "little season" might be is not known. LDS historian Ivan J. Barrett put it this way in 1973: "How long a 'little season' might be no one knew...a person was considered a virtual apostate who dared say they would not be restored to Zion in five years or ten at the most. The history of the church shows that the 'little season' has extended more than a century and a quarter later; yet the redemption of Zion is still a cherished doctrine of the Church of Jesus Christ of Latter-day Saints and every believing member is certain of its reality."[50]

As for the expulsion from Zion [Jackson County] there are today four possible theories, or variations thereof, which prevented the incoming Mormons from residing amiably with their neighbors. They are presented as follows:

1. Joseph must have erred in naming western Missouri as the new Zion. There were many places including New York and Ohio where the saints faced persecution, but none as formidably as here on the edge of civilization where cultures could not have been more prone to clash. Missouri was settled mostly by Southerners bringing slaves with them. According to the *World Book Encyclopedia*, a census taken in 1820 showed 10,222 slaves and there were undoubtedly many more by 1831 when the Mormons showed up to begin buying land for their "New Jerusalem." The Missourians were well aware that the Latter-day Saints taught "free agency," were adamantly opposed to slavery as practiced in the South and would vote against them in any matter of keeping slaves. For that matter, the Missourians feared anyone and everyone advocating abolition, including those flocking to the Kansas region to the west, almost certain to soon enter the Union as anti-slave under the Missouri Compromise.

   In addition, the Book of Mormon taught that the Indians or

"Lamanites" were a chosen people of God, similar to Israelites of the Old Testament. Missourians who fought battles with Osage and other Indians over territorial rights, before removing them to reservations westward, were determined not to relinquish their lands. They looked upon the native Americans with great distrust. Now here came these Mormons claiming the Indians to be a "chosen people of God," trying to proselyte them and accord them a place of equality in decent society.

Furthermore, western Missouri was the nation's western frontier for jumping off into the wilderness, the trailhead for Oregon and Santa Fe trails, and had until recently been a primary market for the fur trade. It was a natural gathering place for what many called "border ruffians," plus fugitives of the law who resented government or other restrictions. Thus, the Missourians' philosophical views were bound to come into conflict with the Mormon immigrants no matter the latter's diligence in being circumspect as per their religious instruction.

Such a view seems to have determined the course of several church members at the time, including Lyman Wight. Settling before most saints arrived in Missouri, the enterprising Wight tilled ground near what is now known as Adam-Ondi-Ahman (said by Joseph Smith to be site of the Garden of Eden) and likely planned to live there the remainder of his days. But when persecution increased, Wight did not abide it and separated himself from the church, letting other members fend for themselves. Little was heard from him again. Conclusion: the Mormons should have never attempted to settle in western Missouri in the first place amid its brigand brand of backwoodsmen. It was like sending lambs among ravenous wolves.

2. All of the above differences between Mormons and Missourians were true enough. But Joseph was carrying out the Lord's will, via revelation, in sending the saints onto sacred ground, even the Garden of Eden. (See D&C 116:1.)[51] In carrying out God's will, Joseph was as much disturbed about the calamities in Jackson County as anyone. His letters to western Missouri do, indeed, indicate much sensitive concern for their safety. No matter how sacred the ground, however, their enemies, acting under the principle of God's free agency to man, prevailed over the saints at this time.

3. The saints "polluted the land of their inheritance" as warned in D&C 103:14; they did not deserve the land the Lord had

preserved for them. If the Children of God had obeyed His commandments in righteousness, they would not have been driven from Zion.

In his Autobiography, Parley P. Pratt suggested as much (see p. 96): "This revelation [to not pollute their inheritance in Jackson County/Zion] was not complied with by the leaders of the church in Missouri as a whole, notwithstanding many were humble and faithful. Therefore, the threatened judgment was poured out to the uttermost..." Pratt did not specify here how the saints might have failed to qualify.

The only antithesis to Pratt's statement is this question: Is there anything the saints could have done, given their different religious beliefs, to avoid the wrath of the people who then inhabited western Missouri? If the saints had been deemed worthy (against an adamant foe) would God then have wiped the region clean, as occurred in the Old Testament with Joshua and the Children of Israel when they occupied their Promised Land at Jericho?

Whatever the answer to this difficult rhetorical question, David Patten, later deemed a martyr in the Battle of Crooked River, was willing to fight with guns and weapons for the right of the saints to remain. Patten was highly praised by Joseph Smith for his valiant service to the cause of the saints. Despite these heroic efforts, however, the saints didn't qualify for "Zion" as had Enoch before them.

4. It was not meant that Zion should be literally established in Jackson County in the 1830s; the saints were expected to set the "groundwork" for a future Zion. They were being tested to eliminate the chaff from the wheat. Those who proved worthy would deserve a Zion sometimes in the future.

There is some indication of the latter view in the 43rd Section of the D&C which reads: "Ye cannot behold with your natural eyes, for the present time, the design of your God concerning those things which shall come hereafter, and the glory which shall come after much tribulation. For after much tribulation come the blessings...And also that you might be honored in *laying the foundation and in bearing record of the land upon which the Zion shall stand*" [author's italics].

These verses may not have been fully understood at the time given. Not by Edward Partridge and the body of the church, quite possibly not by Joseph Smith himself. For that matter, the verses may not be fully understood today and perhaps won't be until the Millennium. The same is true of another Zion, that in Israel where the Jews were invited by the British government to gather in 1948 only to find the "Promised Land" they looked forward to occupying in peace in heavy dispute. Even today, despite various treaties and agreements, an uneasy cloud rests over the head of those who occupy the Holy Land.

Early persecution against the Children of Israel by the Assyrians and Romans as well as other people is well documented. But though physically abused, the faithful were repeatedly told they would triumph spiritually if enduring to the end. Those who opposed God would have to suffer at a later date for their evils.

From his actions, it would appear Edward held to Conclusion No. 2, i.e. complete faith in the prophet's explanation of Zion. Edward visited Joseph during the Zions Camp march with a report which indicated no loss of trust in Missouri/ Zion, besieged though it be. The prophet recorded it this way, according to the Documentary History of the Church, p. 95: "We received much information from him [Bishop Partridge] concerning the hostile feelings and prejudices that existed against us in Missouri in all quarters, but it gave us great satisfaction to receive intelligence from him of the union and good feeling that prevailed among the brethren."

This was vintage, emphasize-the-positive, hold-the-faith Edward Partridge. Whatever the problems, and there were seemingly never more during this phase of LDS church history, there is no indication that Edward ever doubted the Missouri/Zion concept. Following expulsion from Missouri, however, it is quite possible that Bishop Partridge leaned toward explanation No. 4.

Based on testimonies given throughout their lives, Edward and Lydia never gave credence to No. 1. No matter how fearful or adverse conditions became in the darkest Missouri period, no member of the Partridge family ever expressed doubt about Joseph being who and what he claimed to be, a prophet of the Latter-day Dispensation. Diaries of Lydia and the children, writing thousands of pages, did not pull any punches in describing the horror of their experiences in Jackson County; yet, they never expressed any belief that Joseph Smith erred on Zion or any other point of doctrine.

One might also profitably ask, "Would any of the saints,

Partridges included, have been better off by renouncing their faith and leaving it after experiencing the abuse they did?" Perhaps physically and materially. Certainly not spiritually, according to Partridge family members later writing about the Jackson County experience. If there were regrets, none were expressed even though Edward Jr. himself wrote nearly 2,000 pages in his nine journals. Much was written about the rich heritage received from his family based on the Missouri period, including the Christ-like manner in which Edward's bore his tarring/feathering experience.

Did the saints ever recover any of their property left behind in Jackson County? Very little. Two members obtained power of attorney from Edward to return and sell lands (while the mobs might destroy homes and crops, it was difficult to destroy the land itself) in Jackson County for $2,700, which was used to benefit the saints in their poverty.[52]

What about the mobbers who drove the saints out? Did they do so with impunity? No. Joseph Smith had recorded in D&C 103:1-2 concerning the saints' plight in western Missouri that..."being driven and smitten by the hands of mine [the Lord's] enemies...I will pour out my wrath without measure in mine own time." It is there 28 years later. The Civil War brought terrible chastisements, even torture and death, for the citizens of Jackson County. No part of the United States suffered more severely and perhaps for as long as did western Missouri, caught halfway in the conflict between North and South. Historian B. H. Roberts recounts many atrocities committed by Union soldiers against pro-slavery Jackson County and attributes it as retribution to treatment earlier given the saints.[53]

Non-Mormon Pearl Wilcox puts it this way: "Independence was a Civil War center...the citizens had been repeatedly subjected to the terrible realities of civil strife and lawlessness. Public meetings were held...to make Independence a neutral spot..." Citizens drew up a treaty with the Federal government to "make compensation...for all property taken or destroyed by U.S. troops. This was the last determined effort...to bring about peace and restore business...their efforts were of no avail and there still remained no sense of security. Daily and nightly robbing continued and no person felt safe in Jackson County."[54]

Saints looking back on their own experience in Jackson County, 1831-34, could say to themselves, "We know how it feels."

end notes, chapter four

1. These are the author's words, based on descriptions of the incident given by Edward Partridge in his unpublished journals, LDS Church Archives, Salt Lake City, UT; also, the description given by Joseph Smith in his Documentary History of the Church, pp. 390-391, and footnotes therein by historian B. H. Roberts.
2. Edward Partridge Journal, LDS Church Archives, Salt Lake City, UT; also Joseph Smith, *Documentary History of Church* 1:390-393.
3. Ibid.
4. The meek shall inherit the Earth," Matthew 5:5, 3 Nephi 12:5. Edward made no effort to escape his captors but bore the pain meekly for righteousness' sake, as did Christ. Interestingly, the name of Edward's perpetrators have been forgotten while the world yet remembers the Christ-like meekness borne by Partridge in this incident.
5. The diaries of Emily and Caroline, written at a later period, unnumbered pages, can be found in the LDS Church Archives, Salt Lake City, UT, in typescript and microfilm records. See "Sources Cited" for description.
6. DHC 1:392-3. Note: little further mention is made in church history about Charles Allen. Suffice it to say he displayed equal courage with Bishop Partridge on this day by refusing to renounce his religious beliefs.
7. Ibid, p. 394.
8. Ibid, p. 394; footnote by B. H. Roberts.
9. For a full account of the anti-Mormon document, see DHC 1:395-400.
10. See DHC 1:396. There is nothing in LDS annals to even slightly suggest the Mormons intended to take Jackson County "by the sword" as was done In Joshua, Ch. Six of the Old Testament. The saints were commanded to acquire the land by legal purchase.
11. Roberts l:334; DHC 1:391-92.
12. Ibid.
13. Ibid.
14. Pearl Wilcox, *Jackson County Pioneers*, p. 127.
15. Emily's diaries, located in the LDS Church History Archives, are listed under several titles, including "Diary of a Young Mormon Girl," "Incidents in the Life of a Mormon Girl," and also "What I Remember." Since there is some repetition in the journals, it may be that duplicate writings were submitted under one or more similar titles. The last entry in Emily's diary appears to be written as late as 1884.

While Emily's writings of the expulsion from Jackson County are eloquent, it should be noted that much of the same language, i.e. "sallied forth" appeared in Joseph Smith's Documentary History of the Church 1:426. Which came first is up to conjecture.

16. DHC, 2:98. This is the same Gen.Doniphan who later refused to execute Joseph Smith, calling it "cold-blooded murder." Doniphan first became acquainted with the saints when secured as part of their legal counsel seeking redress of property in Jackson County. He was ever their friend afterward, clearly going beyond the $250 paid to secure his services.

17. Ivan J. Barrett, *Joseph Smith and the Restoration*, p. 267-9.

18. DHC 1:448-49.

19. Ibid, p. 451.

20. DHC 1:199. Edward placed the southeast cornerstone on July 4, 1838. Also see Ranney, Part II, p. 8.

21. D&C 42:10. This edict from the Lord does not appear to be an indictment against Edward personally. It was just that the job was so important, as was Joseph's calling as prophet, that if the person called couldn't be trusted with the responsibility, someone else must be immediately appointed who could be.

22. June 22, 1834. This revelation came after the Lord had stated (verse 13),"mine elders should wait a little season for the redemption of Zion."

23. Ranney, Part II, p. 7.

24. This religious group, settling in Pennsylvania under the leadership of William Penn, had early established the fact they put their faith in God, not man, to fight their battles. In this, they were pacifists. *World Book Encyclopedia*, Vol. Q, pp. 459-61.

25. This concept was first given by church leaders in 1844. See DHC 6:318. But for Edward Partridge and the saints in 1833, Zion was none other than Jackson County, MO.

26. DHC 1:409.

27. B. H. Roberts summarizes many of these shortcomings of the saints from his point of view in the *Comprehensive History of the Church* 1:318-319.

28. *Autobiography of P. P. Pratt*, pp. 41-45. Pratt had been successful in teaching the native Americans in the area known as Kansas, but Indian agents and other ministers ran them out. Pratt says that , "...we commenced laboring in Jackson County, Mo. among the whites. We were well received and listened to by many; and some were baptized and added to the church."

29. Ibid, p. 93.

30. Roberts, pp. 329-331.

31. DHC 1:339. Letter of instruction to Jared Carter from Joseph Smith.

32. See Bruce R. McConkie, *Mormon Doctrine*, p. 158

33. *Wilford Woodruff*, edited by M. F. Cowley, p. 45, includes a lengthy description of Woodruff's role in the Law of Consecration.

34. Ibid, p. 150.

35. Wilcox, *Jackson County Pioneers*, pp. 50-51
36. Based on Joseph Smith's statement, repeated by Wilford Woodruff and others, that Bishop Partridge had "no guile," it is the author's conclusion that Edward looked for the same in others, most particularly clergymen, and would be severely disappointed in their displaying unChrist-like hate and anger.
37. Wilcox, p. 36
38. W. Z. Hickman, pp. 167-183
39. Wilcox, pp. 38-39.
40. Ibid, p.94. While such Missouri histories appear to Latter-day Saints today as hypocritical, or even farcial, it should be remembered that Hickman did not live during the 1830-39 "Mormon period" written about. Hickman must rely on the writings of those who did.
41. Ibid, pp 184-85.
42. "Long Journal of Edward Partridge," LDS Church Archives, Salt Lake City, UT
43. *World Book Encyclopedia*, Vol. Q-R, p. 186
44. Malachi 3:1-3. III Nephi 24:2-3
45. D&C 128:24. This is not a revelation given to Joseph Smith but rather an epistle written by him to the church.
46. Roberts, pp. 370-71
47. D&C 45:66
48. *Journal of Mormon History*, Fall, 1996, "Sidney Rigdon and Me," p. 149.
49. D&C 100:13
50. Barrett, p. 290, with reference to remarks by LDS historian Andrew Jenson, *Historical Record*. See "Sources Cited" for references to the latter.
51. *See also R. K. Young, As a Thief in the Night*, p. 77.
52. Ivan J. Barrett, *Joseph Smith and the Restoration*, p. 421.
53. Roberts, 1:547-59.
54. Wilcox, p. 332. Interestingly, according to Wilcox, Jackson County residents even agreed to compromise and show no further sympathies for the pro-slave South, yet could not effect peace. Thus, even in capitulation, they were no more successful in achieving peace than the non-compromising Mormons of an earlier era.

chapter five

Steadying the Ark

When driven from their Zion, Eliza Partridge portrays the ordeal this way:[1] "We traveled three miles and camped on the banks of the river [Missouri] under a high bluff. Rain poured down in torrents...*this was the first night I had ever spent out of doors* (author's italics). Next day we crossed the river into Clay County. Here my father laid up some house logs and stretched a tent on them so we could stay there 'till he could go finish a house. The weather was very cold but we were in the woods where we could have plenty of fires. When my father had done what he could to help the brethren across the river, he with others went out to see if he could find some houses to move into, as there was already snow on the ground. He found a miserable old house that we could occupy. He and a brother named John Corrill moved their families into this house..."

Caroline wrote in her journal that poisonous snakes were sometimes found among their boxes on the dirt floor.

W. W. Phelps wrote Joseph shortly after the expulsion, "The condition of the saints is lamentable and affords a gloomy prospect. No regular order can be enforced [presumably this included the United Order] nor any usual discipline be kept up...we cannot hear from one another oftener than we do from you...I should like to know what the honest in heart can do?" Phelps importunes the prophet for help in finding clothing, food, the necessities of life. On a more positive bent, he adds that in spite of this, the saints seek "to do the will of God." There are "some rebellious" among the members but some saints are as "immovable as the everlasting hills."[2]

The Partridges would prove to be such saints, as were the Corrills. It was John Corill who had been Bishop Partridge's first counselor and who had baptized Eliza. The two families were initially fortunate enough to take flight into Clay County where mixed sympathies allowed the refugees in. Those fleeing into Van Buren County found only hostility and were quickly driven out. But it wouldn't be long before they were treated similarly in Clay County.

In his history of the church, Joseph Smith explained the exodus from Zion this way:

> "On the [nights of] the 5th and 6th of November, women and children fled in every direction from the merciless mob. One party fled to the prairie...other parties fled to the Missouri River and took lodging for the night where they could find it. During this dispersion of the women and children, parties of the mob were hunting the men, firing upon some, tying up and whipping others, and pursuing others with horses for miles. Thursday, Nov. 7, the shores of the MIssouri River began to be lined on both sides of the ferry with men, women and children...some in tents and some in the open air, around their fires, while the rain descended in torrents. Husbands were inquiring for their wives and women for their husbands; parents for children and children for parents...the scene was indescribable...the scene would have melted the hearts of any people on earth"...save it would appear, the mobbers of Jackson County.[3]

Somehow, looking at the event in modern times, even Latter-day Saints are prone to take the attitude that... *"these were pioneers. They were used to hard times. It would be more difficult for us today."* But the journals of Eliza and her sisters indicate that the expulsion from Zion was as brutal and traumatic then as if a Mormon today, perhaps a missionary, found him/her self in a foreign country, expelled by insurgents into wildlands survival with winter coming on.

Let not the distance of time lull one into thinking being thrust to the elements was somehow routine. Edward was not known as a particularly physically robust, Daniel Boone type of cowboy or lumberjack. Lydia was accustomed to a fine home and genteel surroundings. There was nothing in the girls' past, enjoying material comforts in Painesville, to prepare them for such an event. Edward Jr. of course, was less than a year old at the expulsion, and would be an extra burden for Lydia.

In writing of this traumatic time, when even good saints began murmuring against church leaders, Edward showed his love for the prophet by writing a letter with the salutation: "Beloved Brother Joseph..." Describing the situation in Clay County, Edward, always the optimist, says..."The Lord for the most part has given us very favorable weather." At a later period, Partridge descendent Albert R. Lyman wrote that his research showed many saints becoming disaffected with Joseph, blaming him for their ill reception, receiving their own "revelations" about where Zion should be. If Joseph was a prophet, why couldn't he foresee the problems? Yet Lyman points out that there is "not the slightest sign of bitterness" in Bishop Partridge's lengthy letter to Joseph during one of the most difficult times in church history.[4]

Even in the best of weather, however, there must have been little sleep, for there was no way of knowing if mobbers followed Mormon tracks with further mayhem in mind. As the Partridge journals point out, building open fires could keep one warm, but it made the refugees rather easy targets if enemies pursued. For the moment, they didn't.

Cooking in the Partridge-Corrill abode was shared in a small fireplace with pots and pans, for as Eliza writes at a later time, "for there were no stoves then." She also mentions a shower of stars in the Heaven during the first nights of flight, which Eliza suggested could be a show of divine strength "to frighten our enemies." It was a phenomenon so striking as to be mentioned in many histories of late 1833, including that of Joseph Smith. The Prophet wrote that he took the heavenly fireworks as a sign to let them know God was mindful of the saints' dilemma.[5]

Edward was likely much frustrated in the saints' unsettled condition, for living the Law of Consecration was obviously impossible at this time. Edward wrote in several hymns of his yearning for a Zion living the celestial commandment of consecration, but there was no hope for the immediate present. In the above letter, as Phelps explains, any "order" or discipline as to carrying out assigned church duties was nigh impossible. The saints went into Clay County knowing their destiny, as outlined in revelation, was to ultimately return to Jackson County. But how long were they to remain here and indeed, how long might the local residents even allow them the "temporary refuge" they sought? How comfortable should they attempt to get? It was difficult to know where trusted friends might be located, let alone find meaningful social life. Church services, the partaking of the sacred sacrament, might be conducted in clusters of a few families, but never in a manner too conspicuous to the Missourians which might arouse their suspicions. The same might be interpreted as conniving against non-Mormon neighbors. The scene somewhat resembled Russian Orthodox Christians, before fall of the Iron Curtain in the Soviet Union, whose meetings might be allowed, yet were viewed with apprehension by those in power.

As for such niceties as the Partridge girls wearing fine apparel, at an age when they would normally be thinking of such things, perhaps on Sunday, the same might as well be thoughts from another planet. But then, when one seeks mere survival, sacrificing further quality of life might not seem so difficult.

Edward and Lydia's descendent Ruth Louise Partridge has written of this time in her novel, *Other Drums*.[6] In it she depicts the family as living barely above an animal existence, which could be close to the truth. Ruth seems unduly harsh, however, about the Missouri experience: "Another morning and Lydia lying wide-eyed in the gloom. Edward was dead. She was dead. They were all dead and gone to an eternal hell." This is mere speculation, of course, yet a perception of one Partridge descendent. Ruth Louise also depicts Lydia as a dutiful wife but questioning her husband whether Joseph was inspired in sending the family from a comfortable Ohio home to live from day to day like fugitives. It was a period, indeed, as Ruth Louise expresses, when some of the distressed saints began to question the prophet's judgment in sending them to Missouri. But her reference to Lydia seems little short of disservice; in truth, Lydia never hints, even in her later years, of feeling she was deceived in heeding the call to "Zion." Nor does any member of the family. All of the children remained steadfast to the new faith their parents embraced, although not without what appears to be emotional scarring on young minds. It would seem a tribute by mainstream LDS standards, however, to family leaders Edward and Lydia, so far as is known, that they encouraged not the slightest murmuring against church or prophet to escape their lips.

Partridge descendent A.R. Lyman points out that the Missouri ordeal was particularly trying to the Partridge girls. Eliza destroyed the first diary she kept.[7] Lyman concludes he does not know why she might have destroyed this diary, but one can easily conjecture that the emotions she felt as a young girl she later chose to "clean up" with more mature reflection. Thinking was one thing, recording them for posterity another. Historian L. L. Ranney suggests that Eliza destroyed the original because she had written "too freely."[8] Today's followers of church history can only lament the loss of her first thoughts about the Missouri years. They appear to represent the candid but not candy-coated feelings of her child and teen years.

Being removed a century and a half hence, it would be difficult to comprehend how much the prayers and testimonies of the Partridges daily sustained them during this trying period. Caroline wrote that when her older sister, Eliza, was gone that she went into a nearby corn field to pray for the family's survival.[9] The entire experience during this period would, of course, be utter misery if not engaged in a greater cause than themselves. With the gospel of Jesus Christ, it seemed Edward and Lydia, and later their children, took the attitude that they had no more right to be sheltered from adversity than did the Saviour himself when placed at the disposal of Roman soldiers. If Edward yet felt as he did when tarred and feathered barely a year before, he expressed no malice in his heart for the oppressors, considering them less spiritually enlightened with latter-day insight. Where more was given, more was expected. It wasn't a time that one wanted to remember, certainly. But in looking back on it some quarter of a century later, Lydia says: "This [Jackson County] was the beginning of the persecutions of the saints in Missouri, but my faith never failed me; instead it grew stronger in the latter-day work."[10]

Nevertheless, that faith would be severely tested. Ruth Louise was probably right in saying that one reason the Mormons were hated was because of their industry, being willing among the South-oriented Missourians "to do the work of n——s." She also suggests in energetic and lively dialogue that despite any lack of appropriate wearing apparel for her daughters, Lydia noted they were "growing pretty," and "being noticed by the Missouri boys." But it wouldn't require much imagination to say that nothing would be more reprehensible to Edward and Lydia than to have the sons of mob enemies paying social visits to their daughters. History does not record such a thing happening, nor could it be likely in any event, for the saints were soon forced out of Clay County and did not know from week to week where their next home might be. Much of the time, they and other church members attempted to keep their whereabouts unknown so as to avoid further mob depredations.

If happiness is having a comfortable and permanent home, free to come and go in safety, having a known schedule of activities upon which to focus one's energies and ambitions, the family of Edward and Lydia would clearly be in dire arrears. They sorely needed outside assistance, but must remain in deep silence that they belonged to that despised sect known as Mormons. If they found themselves in the wilderness, they were safer from immediate harm; yet as such, they were more subject to the elements and pillaging of wild animals.

What did Missourians later think of the Mormons in Clay County? Interestingly, one history of Clay County[11] describes the year 1833 with these two terse sentences: "Many Mormons came into Clay County from Jackson County. Meetings were held to get rid of them."

The chapter says more of the Mormons but emphasizes the county's "hospitable" citizenry. In 1834, the county's first courthouse was... "warmed by fireplaces... Liberty had a very brilliant social life as officers [from nearby Ft. Leavenworth] came from the fort to enjoy the southern hospitality of Clay County's chief town."

The Mormons had seen enough of Missouri's "Southern hospitality." Even years later, they were merely recorded as an unwanted blip on the screen of Clay County's history. There was one section in the history on early churches which states, "...the relations between these denominations [early settlers] has been amicable and cooperative. The chief exception to this was the opposition to the Mormons and this was chiefly economical and political."[12]

However, the list of grievances issued by those in Jackson County in expelling the Mormons were not political-economic so much as religious. They would remain so throughout the entire Missouri period. For example, the saints had not lived in Clay

County but a few months when one Rev. Riley, a Baptist priest, "made a hot speech" against the Mormons and declared, "The Mormons have lived long enough in Clay County; and they must clear out, or be cleared out." A Mr. Turhman, the moderator of a meeting to discuss the "Mormon problem" probably bought the saints some times by stating, "Let us honor our country and not disgrace it like Jackson County. For God's sake, don't drive away the Mormons. They are better citizens than many of the old inhabitants."[13] Nevertheless, the meeting ended in turmoil as local residents debated whether to allow the refugees to remain.

The question must be asked, "When will a non-Mormon Missouri source provide the world with an honest portrayal of the brutal depredations heaped upon Mormons (however peculiar or objectionable their beliefs) in the period 1833-39?

One of the most favorable histories of the Mormons (some might say biased in that Alexander Majors lived 1869-79 in Great Salt Lake City) that this author has seen by a non-Mormon was written by one of three partners in the Pony Express venture of Majors, Russell and Waddell. Majors says he lived for a short time in the Show-me State during the Latter-day Saint troubles. He got some things wrong about LDS history, such as saying the Missourians attacked the Mormons at "Horn's Mill" but appeared to sincerely seek out the truth in *My Seventy Years on the Frontier*. In his book, Majors says that western Missouri was initially "settled by a poor and illiterate people, although self-sustaining." He writes, "Nothing of very great note occurred in the county of Jackson, after the cyclone of 1826, until the year 1830 when five Mormon elders made their appearance in the community and commenced preaching..."[14] The Mormons believed that Jackson County was "the center of the Earth. This is the place where the Garden of Eden was located, in which Adam and Eve resided...and this is where Jesus Christ is to make his appearance."

A man who advocated strong Christian principles for his Pony Express riders as well as freighters on the trail to Santa Fe, Majors stated in his book published in 1893: "In that day and age it was considered blasphemous or sacrilegious for anyone to claim that they had met angels... and the religious portion of the community was incensed..." Majors referred to speeches by Sidney Rigdon, in which Rigdon talked of going to the "Third Heaven" and "meeting God

Almighty face to face."[15] Majors considered this statement highly inflammatory to the Missourians and he is undoubtedly correct.

Clannishness of Mormons, asserts Majors, made them odious to neighbors. The Mormons also "had a melancholy look," whatever that might mean. "They [the Mormons] claimed that God had given them the locality and that others [non-Mormons] would be crushed out, for this was the Mormon's Promised Land and they had come to possess it. The Lord had sent them there and would protect them against any odds...first man who touched the building [Phelp's Printing Office in Independence] would be paralyzed and fall dead upon the ground." While acknowledging this proved untrue, Majors gives it as his opinion that the atrocities against the Mormons simply strengthened the latter's' resolve, as it has with many religious organizations [say, for example, the Jews] ever since time began. This greater resolve would tend to make non-Mormons in Clay County have reason to feel even more uneasy about the Mormons than when they were in Jackson County to the south.

Majors says he could not find, nor anyone else he checked with, any Jackson County record indicating any Mormons guilty of committing a single crime. "Whatever the Mormons obtained was by their own industry. The Mormons simply received a revelation that was not in accord with the religious denominations...of the time." Other reasons were given by some, but asserts Majors, "I was there, and the sole reason the Mormons were evicted was religious." Majors says that things changed after the Civil War. The Mormons could have returned to Missouri in 1893 and been "laughed at" rather than precipitating mob violence.

Majors says that it was his understanding that a ferry which sunk on the Missouri with many local mobbers as they chased the Mormons during the Zion's Camp period was due to a hole drilled in the flatboat by the ferryman. But since the latter, too, drowned, the report may bear little truth. The fact is that many Missourians considered such rumors to be true; these stories circulated in Clay County as they had in Jackson. Rumors had flown about since 1830 that the Mormons were "going to get even" by destroying Independence; the Mormons in Clay County yet found themselves reviled and feared in similar fashion.

It is with incredulity that one reads in Edward's diary of 1835 that he left his family during the unrest in Clay County for a mission to the Eastern States. Whether he was called directly by the Prophet, or simply felt a compulsion to share a burning testimony of the Restoration with people in another place, Edward soon left his family in God's hands. Eliza says, "He was convinced that the Lord had set up a kingdom here on Earth and when the Lord called, he must obey. He showed his faith by his works."[16]

Edward's first diary entry says, "I started from my home in Clay County on the 27th of January...was joined by Bro.Thomas B. Marsh as a partner in the ministry...snowed all day," and then a frequent entry, "...tried for a meeting but could not get one." Elders Partridge and Marsh traveled across Illinois where they saw Indian mounds and wondered about their connection to the Book of Mormon people. Entries for the next several months, pages 6-50 in his diary,[17] show they were welcome in the home of a sympathetic Baptist, at least until they introduced the Book of Mormon. Then, they were turned out of doors into the cold night by a Mr. Gruel who said he "hated to do so." They found lodging a mile away. At one branch where members were "having difficulty," ostensibly in getting along with one another, a diplomatic Edward said "I attended to the investigation, did not decide the case but concluded to take the minutes to Kirtland and if right, lay the case before the high council." He said he was "really glad" to see Elder Isaac Morley join them at this branch. The precise reason for this emotional interjection, somewhat unusual in Edward's writings, is not explained, but it is likely he welcomed help in solving problems among the branch's quarreling members. At another branch, Edward "tarried with them one day and instructed them respecting their duty."

Edward reported at this point that non-members often believed the elders' preaching or seemed to, "though none joined." There was one notable exception. "We were asked by a young man with tears in is eyes if we would go the water and baptize him." This was Perregreen (Perregrine) Sessions who was to become a prominent member of the church in Utah. Edward took time at this point to express feelings about the scenery: "There were two peaks [in the White Mountains] which looked majestic." Edward stayed one night with a sister, "Widow Dow," but he does not report if he attempted to preach the gospel to her, or if so, the results.

Elder Partridge continued to New York State and eventually to Palmyra, where he visited the Hill Cumorah, then pushes on to Painesville, Ohio. He summarizes his five months' mission there as follows: "Traveled about 2,000 miles, held [in company with Elder Morley] about 50 meetings, preached 32 sermons, and gave some half dozen exhortations...we baptized three."

In Kirtland, Edward wrote enthusiastically about being among friends and attended grammar school, studied Hebrew, preached, and attended meetings "to regulate the house of the Lord," the Kirtland Temple. He now wrote longer entries in his diary about joining the Prophet Joseph and the brethren and "being anointed with Holy oil." He revels in a rich spiritual experience within the temple: "We were blessed with the outpouring of the Holy Ghost and shouted hosanna to the most high...spoke in tongues, blessed... by the Most High God." He says the Prophet Joseph "conferred the benefits of Heaven upon us." Edward adds that some of the brethren reported having visions and seeing angels, "as they declared unto us." Edward does not make such a claim but mentions several who do during this special time in LDS history. B. H. Roberts points it out as a period when the saviour and many ancient prophets appeared to the saints. "...the reported visions and other spiritual manifestations therein created a sensation throughout northern Ohio."[18] Edward, an eye-witness to this outpouring of the spirit in the dedication of the Kirtland Temple, appears to be rather conservative in his remarks but likely felt the events were so personal for himself and other saints that few additional adjectives were needed.[19] The first bishop of the church was not one to multiply words.

Before leaving, Edward participated in the ordinance of washing of feet in the name of the Lord... "we then partook of bread and wine...prophesied and shouted hosannas...the meeting lasted until daylight." On Thursday church leaders met again to accommodate those who could not get in for the Sunday ceremonies. "This meeting rather surpassed the Sunday meeting both in length and goodness," wrote Edward.

While here, Bishop Partridge also received his endowment "with power from on high" as previously "called and chosen" by the Prophet Joseph.[20]

All of the foregoing indicates the spiritual strengthening experienced by Edward. He would need it all to face the trials which yet lie ahead in Missouri.

Following their missions, the Prophet Joseph says in his history that he received revelation stating the Lord was "well pleased" with Edward Partridge and Isaac Morely "because of the integrity of their hearts in laboring in my vinyard, for the salvation of the souls of men..."[21] Of the talks given by Elders Partridge and Morely, Joseph adds high praise for two humble men who themselves say little of the event: "These discourses were well adapted to the times in which we live, and the circumstances under which we are placed. Their words were words of wisdom, like apples of gold in pictures of silver, spoken in the simple accents of a child, yet sublime as the voice of an angel. The Saints appeared to be much pleased with the beautiful discourses of these two fathers in Israel."[22]

Joseph adds: "Myself and the principal heads of the church, accompanied the *wise men of Zion* [author's italics] namely Edward Partridge and his counselors, Isaac Morely and John Corrill and...W. W. Phelps as far as Chardon; and after staying with them all night, blessed them in the morning and returned to Kirtland."[23] No more is said of Thomas Marsh, although he began the missionary work with Edward. History records that Marsh would soon leave the church and make life extremely difficult for his fellow saints by telling lies about them to Gov. Boggs.

Before leaving the region, Edward preached to a congregation of Methodists and then headed eagerly homeward to family members. Arriving in Clay County, he "found them well. I think I felt as thankful as ever I did in being permitted to again rejoice with my family."

Edward would be home but a few weeks when trouble raised its unwelcome head. It was not entirely unexpected, for Edward with other of his brethren had scouted lands northward for possible future occupancy. The closing pages of his diary include these entries precisely as he wrote them: "On the 29th June the people of Liberty held a meeting and stepped in, as they say, between the mob & us, they drew up a preamble and resolutions amounting to this, that we had taken refuge with them in our distress when driven from Jackson Co, that they treated us kindly at that time, that of late some had become hostile to us in consequence of the emigration to this Co. & the many stories that were afloat about us as a people, none of which did they pretend were true, but from the great excitement which prevailed, to escape a civil war, they proposed to us to stop the emigration to this Co. immediately to have the late emigrants leave soon..."

The "resolution" allowed Mormons with 40 acres or more land to stay until they could dispose of their property. Of course, with locals initially buying nothing, the pressured saints would have to sell for less, if indeed, they received any remuneration at all. Edward says he met with Bros. Morely, Corrill, Marsh and E. Higby to comply with their neighbors request that they move on. "We gave them to understand that we wanted peace and were willing to make sacrifices, to keep it, if it were necessary."

On July 1, writes Edward:

We the elders of the church a goodly number met, and made out a preamble and resolution amounting to this, that we would endeavor to comply with what, they had said was the only way to save the Co. from a civil war, that is we would leave the Co. agreeably to their advise [sic]." This was "received with satisfaction" by the mob and "it [the mob action threatened) gradually died away.

The beleaguered saints might have taken some solace in this, for they could at least depart calmly, as families, in sharp contrast to their forced flight from Jackson County.

Edward's diary, which ended in mid-sentence "along the western line of the..." was the last known personal journal that he kept, although he was to later write much in seeking redress from the State of Missouri.

Parley P. Pratt sheds additional light on the early Missouri experience. In spite of the above persecutions, he says, "...great blessings had been poured out" on the saints. "Many great and marvelous things were manifested." The saints received spiritual strength in their time of need, but " a meeting was held in Clay County to deprive us our citizenship." Pratt extols the saints for sticking together in their time of need, and paints a brighter picture than some who portrayed this period. He says that when he and Phelps were elected by the local brethren to carry the message of what was happening in Missouri to Kirtland that the saints, who were penniless," somehow managed to find him a horse and saddle and warm clothing for the journey. Like the other saints, "robbed and plundered." Said Pratt, "I was entirely destitute... But there was much sweet communion concerning the things of God and the mysteries of his kingdom."[24]

Joseph Smith records the "resolution" of the Clay County citizens as follows: "Report: It is apparent to every reflecting mind that a crisis has arisen in this county, that requires the deep, cool, dispassionate consideration, and immediate action of every lover of peace, harmony and good order...the clouds of civil war are rolling up their fearful masses, and hanging over our devoted country. Solemn, dark and terrible...they [the Mormons]...were driven from Jackson County...like Noah's dove without a resting place...Their destitute and miserable condition at that inclement season of the year excited the deep sympathies and philanthropic and hospitable citizens of this county...notwithstanding the thousand reports...charging them with almost every crime known to our country [yet] they were received with friendship and treated with toleration and often with remarks of peculiar kindness..." Then the bottom line: the Mormons were to later "leave us in peace as they found us. That period has now arrived."

The report says that as more and more Mormons moved in, many from Ohio, "duty requires" the citizenry "to demand that the Mormons depart." The report adds that "...the ignorant and impudent among them" claim "this country is destined by heaven to be theirs... received and looked upon...as convincing proofs that they intend to make this country their permanent home..."

While the foregoing was not technically true, since Jackson County was clearly the planned permanent Mormon home, it is certain that the saints would like to have settled close to Zion for as long as possible in the hopes of some day being repatriated.

In a second meeting, the citizens urged "keeping the peace toward the Mormons as good faith, justice, morality and religion require." It was even suggested that the citizenry raise money to help the Mormons in their move, although there is no record of the latter happening. The citizens suggested the Mormons move to Wisconsin, or somewhere (anywhere but here) "where they will be, in a measure, the only occupants."[25] For modern followers of LDS history, it might be likened to the last scenes of *Fiddler on the Roof* where the Russian Jews were pushed from their homes, yet allowed to go in peace *so long as they went quickly*.

A letter from the leaders of the church in Kirtland emphasized this point: "We are sorry the disturbance has broken out, but we do not consider it our fault." The letter advises the saints not to be first aggressors..."go in peace... observe the principles and above all, show yourselves men of God."[26]

Gov. Dunklin wrote his usual letter to the saints sympathizing with them but suggesting they must have done something inflammatory to ire their neighbors so in Clay County as they had done in Jackson. It is not clear whether the saints even bothered to answer this time to a chief executive high on principle but so lacking in courage to take meaningful action.

Eliza sums it up this way: "...the people among whom we had been living began to feel uneasy about us...they [the citizens] found what they thought was a good place in what was later named Caldwell County. Our people bought land there... thinking to live in peace by themselves...they wanted to get clear beyond where they would be offensive to anybody."

Caldwell County was soon established by the Missouri legislature as "a place for the saints to go, a Mormon County..." Here, as the Missourians said, the saints could be "off by themselves." Expediting the favorable legislation was Alexander Doniphan, prominent in many Missouri affairs, who believed the saints never deserved the treatment foisted on them by his peers. But a whirlwind was to descend in the new county on Edward Partridge and his family, as well as the other church members. Its dark fury made Jackson and Clay counties seem like a rapidly-passing rain squall.

end notes, chapter five

1. Eliza Partridge journal, LDS Church Archives, Salt Lake City, UT. See also Albert R. Lyman's "Edward Partridge Family Journal," 1954, unpublished typescript, pp. 21-22.
2. Documentary History of Church, 1:457, recorded by Joseph Smith Dec. 15, 1833. In this letter, Phelps makes it clear he doesn't believe the saints can return to Zion unless God or the President "rules out the mob." Some have criticized Phelps for appearing to complain but he simply seems confused about what to do.
3. DHC 1:436-7. Some saints, including W. W. Phelps, had complained that Joseph was not aware how severe the saints' plight was in Missouri, and for a time this might have been true. There is little doubt, however, at the time Joseph began writing this history in the late 1830s that he understood he severity of the Missouri saints' ordeal in some detail.
4. Lyman, p. 23, based on writings of Eliza, Caroline and other members of the Partridge family, as well as Joseph Smith.
5. Eliza's journal, repeated by Lyman, p. 22. See also DHC 1:439-40.
6. One may say that a novel has no place in serious history, but the manuscript quite likely reflects the thinking of others studying the Mormon's plight in Missouri. Ruth Louise's theme is replete with lamentations for church-caused injustices. The Partridges, however, emerge in her novel as fully determined to abide by principles of the Restored gospel, as is attested in the Partridge journals themselves.
7. Lyman, EPFJ, p. 29. "Eliza for some reason known only to her, destroyed the first diary she kept..." This was apparently a diary written not only of the Clay County experience but Caldwell County as well, since she also writes of her father being taken to prison which happened after the family moved from Clay County.
8. Ranney, *Our Priceless Heritage*, Part II, "Children of Edward and Lydia Partridge," p. 10.
9. Caroline Partridge Journal. See also Lyman, pp. 24-25. Unfortunately, as Lyman and other Partridges have stated, neither Edward nor Lydia kept a daily diary of this period. One reason was likely a mental mind-set focused on daily survival. It

may also be that Edward and Lydia seemed to have a philosophy of saying nothing at all if you can't say something good.

10. Lydia's writings late in life, as compiled by Lyman, pp. 16-17.
11. *Clay County, Missouri Sesquicentennial Souvenir,* 1822-1972. Interestingly, the authors who slight the Mormons are members of the "Alexander Doniphan Chapter of the American Revolution;" Doniphan was easily the best non-Mormon friend the saints had in Missouri.
12. Ibid, p. 248-9.
13. DHC, 2:97-8; June, 1834.
14. Two chapters about the Mormons encompass pages 43-63. Majors' scholarship on minute matters might be brought in question with references to Haun's Mill as "Horn's Mill." He also stated that Mormons consider Jackson County as "center of the earth," which isn't quite the way Joseph Smith described it. But Majors does present his personal perception of Mormon/Missouri conflicts during the 1830s.
15. See *Doctrine and Covenants,* Sect. 76, particularly verse 21-23. Herein, Rigdon said he saw Christ, and the "glory of God," not God himself, as Majors stated. But Majors got it essentially correct: the Mormon leader Rigdon claimed to have seen deity, which didn't set well with the Missourians.
16. Eliza's diary. See also Lyman, p. 23.
17. Pages 9-31 in the edited diary transcribed by Lyman De Platte, a descendent of Edward Partridge.
18. Roberts, pp. 389-90. See also *Documentary History of the Church* 2: chapters 29 and 30.
19. Edward's style of writing in which he avoids personal opinions might be termed "objective" today. To write with little personal invective is a goal of newspaper writers trained by modern wire services, including the Associated Press. Still, one might wish Edward offered his insights more freely about what it was like to serve with Elder Thomas B. Marsh who would within a few years betray the saints in telling Gov. Boggs the Mormons were the "enemies" of Missouri. (Perhaps he saw nothing out of the ordinary while serving with the man who would soon become president of the Twelve.) Edward also says other members saw visions or angels in the Kirtland Temple, but he did not make such a claim himself.
20. DHC, 2:112.

21. DHC, 2:302-3.
22. Ibid, 2:321. Isaac Morely was to remain a faithful counselor of Bishop Partridge until the latter's death. Edward does not elaborate on the talks which Joseph praises.
23. Ibid p. 436.
24. *Autobiography of Parley Parker Pratt*, pp. 83-4.
25. DHC, 2:452-5.
26. Ibid, pp. 455-6. The letter suggests that if the saints follow these admonitions, the Clay County citizens might later stand by them and come to their assistance. History does not record such an event happening, however.

chapter six

"The Solution to the Mormon Problem"

Bishop Partridge and the other saints would have much reason for rejoicing in moving to Caldwell County. Here, where the Missouri Legislature had designated a new county as a "permanent home" for the Mormons, they would surely find peace. Even the residents of Jackson and Clay counties seemed to look at the arrangement as a means of once and for all settling the "Mormon problem."

The new county was described as "open prairie," with the feeling being among western settlers at the time that if trees couldn't grow there, the soil must not be fertile. It was expressed in the history of Caldwell County as follows: "If the Mormons are willing to go into that prairie country and settle, let them have it and welcome..."[1]

The history added, "The Mormons said, 'If we may be allowed to remain peaceably and enjoy our religion...no matter how wild and unbroken...we will...make it blossom as the rose'."

Concludes the Caldwell history, "Arrangements were soon made. Every Gentile in the proposed new county that could be induced to sell his possessions at a reasonable price was bought out and his place taken by a Mormon." Meantime, it appears to have been verbally understood (such a thing couldn't be legally legislated at this point in Missouri history) that no Mormon was to settle in any other county without consent of settlers already there. Few gave any welcome, except at exorbitant prices.

"It is evident," says historian B. H. Roberts that with the phrase "let them have it and welcome," the Missourians thought this new prairie county "to be worthless."[2] One thing further expediting an exodus into the new county was that some Mormons had already begun settling in a place called Far West, the highest point of land for miles around, and another area known as Shoal Creek. Both were within the new Caldwell boundaries. Nearby was the sacred place named by Joseph Smith as "Adam-ondi-Ahman" (no precise reason for this name was ever given by Joseph Smith) where the prophet said the Garden of Eden had originally been located.[3]

Thus it was that with the blessing of the state of Missouri, Mormons swarmed into Far West. As per Joseph's instructions, they followed closely the plans originally drawn for "Zion" in Jackson County. This included plat by plat, block by block instructions where residences would provide equitable space for all, leaving space for a temple and church buildings. The temple would be a special edifice constructed on "Holy Ground." Proclaimed Doctrine and Covenants 115:7-8 (April 26, 1838): "Let the city Far West be a holy and consecrated land unto me; and it shall be called most holy, for the ground upon which thous standest is holy. Therefore, I command you to build a house unto me, for the gathering of my saints, that they may worship me...and let the beginning be by Fourth of July next...and again (verse 17),...it is my will that the city of Far West should be built up speedily by the gathering of my saints."

This commandment was adhered to by the saints eagerly. By November, 1838, some 5,000 saints, including Joseph Smith and Sidney Rigdon (recently fleeing severe persecution in Kirtland) made it the largest city in western Missouri.

Interestingly, D&C 115 also states in verses 2-6 that Edward Partridge with other church leaders should

> ...arise and shine forth, that thy light may be a standard for the nations. And that the gathering together upon the land of Zion...may be for a defense and for a refuge from the storm..."

Those who took these verses to mean a literal and immediate "refuge" from their enemies would have a shock coming, for it was not long before the Missourians looked once again upon the industry of the Mormons with jealousy and renewed animosity.

With Missouri-Mormon conflicts renewed to and even surpassing former fury, some of the saints had been tried long enough. As Albert R. Lyman put it in on page 29 of his "Edward

Partridge Family Journal"..."In 1837 came a new and terrifying kind of strain, a general apostasy... trusted friends became traitors...no one knew on who to depend. and yet all this was a beginning of what was to befall them in in 1838."

Roberts suggests in his CHC 1:442 that the church members were embarrassed on what course they ought to take, continue to turn the other cheek "seventy times seven," (forever, as Jesus seemed to suggest) or fight back like men? Whichever course of action was correct, should they stubbornly hold to Missouri as Zion, or give up the fight for another day?

Petitions were drawn up to force "weak," or faltering church members out of the state. One such incident followed Sidney Rigdon's "Salt of the Earth" oration at Far West in which he said that "those who have lost their savor should be cast out." Among those leaving at this time were no less than W. W. Phelps and John Whitmer. Gone also in the Quorum of the Twelve by now were John Boynton, Lyman Johnson, Luke Johnson and William M'llelin.

To make matters worse, also defecting were Oliver Cowdery and David Whitmer, two of the original Three Witnesses to the Book of Mormon. Both appeared to grow weary with how the church was dealing with the policy not to sell Jackson County lands they now began to see, amid the renewed conflicts, as unredeemable."[4]

Ironically, however, under Bishop Partridge's "practical" direction, money was received for lost property in Jackson County. Whether the bishop took matters into his own hands in doing so is not clear via any written authority from church headquarters. But the action proved a humane one. The money was used to feed the poor.

The loss of so many once-stalwart church members must have deeply grieved Edward's soul. But the losses did prove one point: past fidelity meant little if you didn't measure up now to mushrooming adversity. The general feeling was that the "loyals," those like Bishop Partridge and Parley P. Pratt, should not be subject to "rotten apples" remaining in the barrel which could spoil all. In most cases, however, one need not suppose these excommunicated brethren were all guilty of serious improprieties such as sexual sins. In most cases they simply seemed flaccid in facing increasing persecution for what had seemed a promised refuge. "Zion" was a vexation many just did not know how to deal with.

With the "fall" of Phelps and Whitmer, a new presidency was appointed in Missouri consisting of Thomas B. Marsh, president, with Brigham Young and David W. Patten as counselors. On the surface, it would seem that with this new "more worthy" presidency, Bishop Partridge might relinquish many previous leadership responsibilities and focus on restoring the Law of Consecration. But it would not be long before Patten would die in conflict with armed mobs at the "Battle of Crooked River" and Marsh would side with the saints' enemies. Edward was again relieved of some responsibilities when the Law of Consecration was disbanded on July 8 and tithing instituted to provide for the temporal welfare of the church. Bishop Partridge must still collect moneys under the new declaration of tithing but the awful burden of taking and distributing lands for each member was for now removed.

Tithing was not, however, defined in D&C Sect. 119 as merely giving one tenth as we know it today. It was to be one-tenth following the saints' *surplus*, although members in Missouri probably had little surplus to give. A key statement from D&C 119 is as follows: "Verily, thus saith the Lord, I require all their surplus property to be put into the hands of the bishop [Edward Partridge] of my church in Zion...and this shall be the beginning of tithing of my people...And after that, those who have thus been tithed shall pay one-tenth of their interest annually; and this shall be a standing law unto them forever..."

Specifically, Edward was now to be the storehouse for all money and/or goods paid under the new Law of Tithing. As such, he was also the person in charge of dispensing it to the needy, of which there were many; it must have been a most difficult decision at that period to ascertain who was more needy than another. At the same time, Edward must maintain accurate accounting of all money, and presumably cattle, chickens or other goods paid in kind.

But Bishop Partridge had other duties as well. On numerous occasions he met in council to quiet accusations made against the prophet and be the peacemaker in defending Joseph and Hyrum. At one hearing, Lyman Wight railed against Oliver Cowdery and W. W. Phelps for selling their property in Jackson County and "denying the faith."[5] Partridge, in fact, presided over a church court brought against Cowdery. On April 12, 1838, Cowdery wrote to Partridge as follows: "I received your note...containing a copy of nine charges preferred against me...I do not charge you, or any other person who differs with me...of being insincere but such difference does exist which I sincerely regret." The letter was sent to Rev. Edward Partridge, Bishop of the Church of Latter-day Saints.[6]

Meantime, the saints were finding opposition to their way of life in Daviess and Carroll counties. At Gallatin, where a preponderance of Mormons attempted to vote, non-Mormons rose in rebellion and a "riot" ensued.[7] This was reported to Boggs, now governor, as a Mormon "uprising." Citizenry elsewhere complained that the Mormons "refused to abide" by Missouri laws, and that they were in insurrection. Boggs called out militia to "put down" these "acts of disloyalty." But two generals, David Atchison and Alexander Doniphan, said they could find no lawbreaking among the Mormons and attempted to inform the governor he was "not in possession of the facts." Atchison objected so strenuously as to be replaced. The general wrote to Boggs:

> I have no doubt your excellency has been deceived by the exaggerated statements of designing or half crazy men. I have found there is no cause of alarm on account of the Mormons; they are not be feared; they are very much alarmed." Atchison emphasized to the governor, "I do not feel to disgrace myself, or permit the troops under my command to disgrace themselves by acting the part of a mob. If the Mormons are to be driven from their homes, let it be done without any color of law and in open defiance thereof.[8]

Boggs, of course, didn't want to hear such insubordination. He saw to it that Atchison was given duties elsewhere. Even when the citizens of DeWitt County sent a message to the governor testifying of the Mormon's willingness to submit to law, the chief executive stated, "The quarrel is between the Mormons and the mob, and they can fight it out!"[9]

Interestingly, Boggs himself called the Missouri agitators a "mob." In receiving this news that they must "fight it out among themselves," weaponry rather than law being their only means of defense, the saints were accused of engaging in an "uprising" as soon as they deployed guns and arms.

Of course, when the mob received word of the governor's actions, they grew much bolder in their depredations. If left in this state of affairs, the Mormons might have become embroiled in a civil war determined solely by the strongest military force. Divine intervention hadn't seemingly appreciably halted the mobbers in the past while exercising their free agency. But the saints' ouster in Missouri was soon hastened by an act of villainy perhaps unequalled in LDS history, tantamount to the defecting of "patriot" Benedict Arnold when he turned spy for the British. Thomas B. Marsh, president of the Quorum of the Twelve, vacated Far West Oct. 18 to make out an affidavit claiming "inside information" that the Mormons planned to burn and destroy local Missouri towns, including Richmond.[10] Why would he testify to such a lie when the Mormons were hiding out just to remain alive against mob persecution? Perhaps Marsh saw nothing but increased persecution ahead and decided to join forces with the enemy in an effort to reduce his own fears.[11]

Boggs responded with much excitement and alarm after seeing this written statement by Marsh, given here in part:

> They have among them a company, considered true Mormons, called the "Danites', who have taken an oath to support the heads of the church in all things that they say or do, whether right or wrong...the Mormons have appointed a company of twelve, called the 'Destruction Company' for the purpose of burning and destroying...and if the people of Clay and Ray made any movement against them, this destroying company were to burn Liberty and Richmond...the Prophet inculcated the notion, and it is believed by every true Mormon that Smith's prophecies are superior to the laws of the land. I have heard the Prophet say that he would yet tread down the enemies and walk over their dead bodies..."

The most damaging part of this statement claims the conspiracy not to be among a few hothead Mormons (a faction calling themselves Danites seeking retribution did exist at this time minus authorization from Joseph Smith), but that the Prophet himself was chief instigator of the threat. Worse, Orson Hyde, up to this point an unwavering church member in many past travails against the church, made out an affidavit stating he knew "much of

Marsh's statement to be true."[12]

Hyde later repented in utter humility at this affront against the saints, saying that he was "afflicted" with darkness. "I sinned against God and my brethren; I acted foolishly. I will not allude to any causes for so doing save one, which was that I did not possess the light of the Holy Ghost."[13]

Marsh was to also repent of his affadivit years later, but the damage was done. Gov. Boggs now had everything he needed to issue his infamous extermination order, in every way illegal against the existing laws of state and country; but the mob was quick to act upon it. The order issued on Oct. 27, 1838, read in part, "The Mormons must be treated as enemies, and must be exterminated or driven from the state if necessary for the public peace — their outrages are beyond all description."[14]

Incredibly, several sentences later, Boggs is no longer intent on driving the Mormon pestilence from the state but in avenging it. Boggs now orders Gen. John B. Clark to join Gen. Doniphan in "intercepting the retreat of the Mormons to the north."[15] This communication with the word *intercept* makes it clear that Boggs sought not only to rid his state of the Mormons but to annihilate them. The governor seems oblivious, however, to the fact that Doniphan, being the stalwart for justice that he was, would never agree to such an order.

But it was clear that Atchison and Doniphan could not dispel the misunderstanding of their fellow Missourians summed up in this statement by Gen. Clark at the surrender of Far West by church leaders: "I am sorry, gentlemen, to see so great a number of apparently intelligent men found in the situation you are; and oh! that I could invoke that Great Spirit, the Unknown God...to make you sufficiently intelligent to break that superstition...that you no longer worship a man!"[16]

Even a supposedly sympathetic Gen. Clark could not understand that the Latter-day Saints devotedly worshipped God, not Joseph Smith and such a speech could only toughen the Mormon will to worship Him in even greater dedication.

That dedication was exemplified in Edward's determination to succeed in the promised land of Missouri. In Jackson County, he stated in an indictment he wrote against the state that he was forced to vacate 2,136 acres of land and two village lots in Independence. "I held the title to 40 acres of land in Clay County." He had five houses and one barn in Caldwell Count, along with 868 acres of land. He had also dug a well and made many improvements in Caldwell County. All of this he was forced to walk away from. On May 15, 1839 Edward figured the total sum of his devotion to remain in Missouri cost him and his family $36,992.00,[17] a vast figure for those times. Obviously, had Edward had been allowed to move directly from Painesville, Ohio to Illinois, as was the case with many of the more industrious saints, he would have been a wealthy man by 1839.

As descendent A. R. Lyman later described it:

when he was confronted again as to the question of what he would retain, this property or his place in the Kingdom, he surrendered them all [his material possessions.]"[18]

According to action of the Missouri legislature, the Mormons were supposed to be allowed to reside in peace in Caldwell County, but Edward made this statement concerning militia activities in Far West: "At different times when I lay down at night I expected to be disturbed before morning." He said Missouri troops milled about the area but he didn't know at any given time if they were there to attack or protect the saints. The mob-militia asked for an audience with the Mormon leaders. "No sooner had they got these men in their possession than they commenced the most hideous shouting and yelling I ever heard...I never before had conceived that it was possible for human beings to make such a hideous noise. They kept us [Edward discloses here that he was one of the leaders taken into custody] guarded...they abused Mr. Isaac Morely...[he] is one of the most peaceable men I ever knew." He was then told by a colonel that some of his men "have got some whiskey" and "I am afraid if any of the Mormons are around that some accident may happen..." The troops then plundered Edward's hay and corn, and burned down the buildings afterward. Naturally, Edward feared even more depredations against his wife and family.

Bishop Partridge was taken not long thereafter, with other Mormon leaders to the jail at Richmond, "guarded by the vilest of the vile."[19] All this happened, of course, after the mobs were given free reign to do as they pleased with the saints following Gov. Boggs' extermination order.

Response of the mob was explained this way by Caroline Partridge in her journal:

> We lived there until the mob came against us again, and took all the leading brethren, including my father, to prison. The mob said they had the governor's orders to kill our people or drive them out of the state. They did kill quite a few, but our leaders agreed to leave the state rather than be exterminated.

That the Missourians meant business had already been displayed at Haun's Mill, not far from Far West, where 17 Mormon men and boys were killed in a brutal attack without warning or provocation of any kind. At least one Missouri history was to claim this massacre as partial revenge of Missourians killed at the Battle of Crooked River.[20]

This is nonsense. The latter was a skirmish with people on both sides being killed, the saints on the defense for their lives.

After Bishop Partridge was taken without due process of law to prison in Richmond, some of his ensuing poor health may well have been caused by emotional stress. He was not known to possess robust physical health to the extent that say, Lyman Wight displayed (the same who later left the church) but the most devastating event of all since leaving Zion in Jackson County almost certainly had to be departing Far West. It, with the temple ground, had been decreed by the Lord as "holy ground." Now the saints must abandon all they held most dear. Morale was to drop even lower when the Prophet himself, brother Hyrum and other church leaders were incarcerated in the Liberty Jail and sentenced to be shot as 1838 came to a close.

During this period Edward wrote a prayer for the beleaguered saints which must go down as one of the most profound and eloquent in all LDS history. Excerpts include (see Appendix for full text):

> Oh Lord, look down in mercy upon thy people, who are afflicted and oppressed. How long oh Lord wilt thou suffer the enemy to oppress thy saints. Destruction hath come upon us

like a wild wind..."

After acknowledging blessings of being preserved from death, the bishop laid it on the line:

> But thou didst suffer the enemy unlawfully to take thy servant, together with scores of others, who drove us like dumb asses from our home in a cold and melancholy time...thou didst suffer the wicked to tyrannize over us, yea the vilest of vile did guard us and treat us like dogs; yet we bore our oppressions without murmuring...but our souls were vexed...for they constantly blasphemed thy holy name.

Edward says the saints were delivered "to some degree" yet death still threatens... "but we are in thy hands, O Lord, and we know that the enemy can go no further in oppressing us than thou dost permit..."[21]

Bishop Partridge later took the lead in writing a petition for redress to the Missouri legislature as the saints made a final effort for justice. This memorial to the legislature, with Edward's name appearing first among the signatories, stands today as meaningful in elaborating the injustices against them as when it was written. After addressing the illegal actions taken against them by Missouri mobs disguised as militia, from Jackson to Caldwell County, excerpts include (see Appendix for complete text):

> In laying our case before your Honorable body, we say that we are willing and always have been, to conform to the Constitution and laws of this state...We ask for the privilege guaranteed to all free citizens of the United States, and of this state, to be extended to us that we may be permitted to settle and live where we please, and worship God according to the dictates of our conscience without molestation. And while we ask for ourselves this privilege, we are willing all others should enjoy the same.[22]

Guided by Gov. Boggs' influence, the legislature appropriated $2,000 for the saints in their duress to help them depart the state, very little of which was ever known to reach the Mormons, and $200,000 to the Missourians who fought against the Mormons for "military expenses." To add insult, the inflammatory statements of Boggs were allowed in the legislative record, while those of the Caldwell County saints were not.[23]

Clearly, after this mockery of justice, there was no way Edward dared trying to make a life for his family in presently-designated "Zion." Even after being released from jail, the mob might at any time return to arrest him. Other church leaders were in the Liberty Jail and mobs were breathing fire on all known sympathizers to the Mormons. Edward departed Far West in the late fall of 1839 and traveled to Quincy, Illinois where he made arrangements for his family to stay with member King Follett. He then sent word for his family to join him in the Illinois refuge.

Family members had up to this time earned a scant living taking odd jobs where no one asked if they were Mormons. For example, Eliza said in her journal that she boarded 30 miles from home, among potential Gentile enemies, to teach school. She was not able to communicate with her family to know if they were yet safe for three months. "Although I did not see anyone I had ever seen before, the Lord watched over me and returned me safely to my parents again. I was at that time about 17 years old."[24]

Now, they must vacate whatever self-reliant financial and emotional security they had managed to gain, and start over once again, throwing themselves upon the mercy of the Lord. Once again, Lydia must make a pilgrimage through unknown territory without her husband, crossing the Mississippi River on both boat and ice. Edward met his family at the river's edge. Says Eliza, "As before, we had to leave most our things behind. The church was scattered with no place of gathering. Harriet and Emily had the ague about a year. I did not have it. I had worn it out..."[25]

In Quincy, the Partridge girls said King Follet proved a true friend and assisted them in every possible way.

Brigham Young, who had already fled with his family to Illinois, inquired of Bishop Partridge what he planned to do to help the poor saints in Missouri find food and refuge. The following is recorded by Joseph Smith in his history:

About this time President Brigham Young proposed to Bishop Partridge to help the poor out of the state. The Bishop replied,

"The poor may take care of themselves, and I will take care of myself."[26] Joseph says Brigham replied, "If you will not help them out, I will."

Historian Ivan J. Barrett says that a "weary" Edward later "expressed regret" for making this statement.[27] In fact, once in Quincy, Barrett says Edward was a key figure in organizing the saints fleeing to Illinois and providing for the poor.[28] If Edward refused to help, it was apparently a temporary lapse from one who had been trying to help the poor and destitute ever since entering Jackson County in 1831 — with little or no success.

As president of the Quorum of the Twelve, Young called a meeting and secured written promises of many of the better-off saints to help the poor migrate to Illinois.[29] Edward's name was not on this list. However, it appears from Barrett's account that Edward was providing relief from the east side of the Mississippi.

While many saints visited Joseph and Hyrum and other church leaders in the Liberty Jail in 1839, the name of Edward Partridge is not mentioned. He had served some time in a Missouri jail himself and likely felt it would be unsafe to return.

Modern day historians were to find many bodies of the saints lying in unmarked graves in Far West. It indicated how quickly most church members hastened from the state without properly designating "hallowed ground."[30] Many bodies were found in an area about one mile west and a quarter mile north of the designated temple site. As one historian noted, the Mormons didn't bury their dead in cemeteries adjacent to churches, like the Protestants do, so it wasn't as easy to find the deceased. Graves were still being discovered into the 1990s.

In his exile from Missouri, Bishop Partridge likely saw more than the loss of home and property; he saw the loss of his sacred leadership role in establishing the saints in Zion.

As for he and his family, they had physically survived Missouri, apparently without feeling any greater imposition than had the Savior or early saints for what they suffered. Yet, the hatred and killing of the mobs, the animosity expressed against all he loved and stood for...all that likely printed an indelible scar upon his soul most difficult to forget. It could scarcely be otherwise.

end notes, chapter six

1. *History of Livingston and Caldwell Counties*, National Historical Co., St. Louis, 1886. See opening pages of Caldwell County.
2. Roberts, 1:418.
3. D&C 107:53-57. See also Old Testament, Daniel, Ch. 7.
4. This statement is not meant to suggest lack of faith in gospel *principles* on the part of either man. They seemed to be in disagreement with church *policy* in dealing with the Missouri problem. To show their fidelity upon church *principle*, neither renounced his testimony in the Book of Mormon nor the original vision in which the pages of the Golden Plates were explained to them, as they stated, by an angel. When efforts were made to restrain them from selling their property in Jackson County, both rebelled against the church directive. See Roberts, 1:430.

    Interestingly, by 1838, it was not considered a loss of faith to obtain money for property lost in Jackson County. Two elders who received a power of attorney from Edward Partridge sold church property in "Zion" for $2,700 to help the poor, according to Ivan J. Barrett, *Joseph Smith and the Restoration*, p. 421.

    Whitmer had other difficulties, namely the Word of Wisdom. He continued to use tea, coffee and tobacco. Roberts, 1:431.
5. DHC, 3:4-5.
6. Roberts, 1:432-4.
7. Roberts, 1:447.
8. Ibid, 1:457-64. Brig. Gen. H. G. Parks also wrote Gov. Boggs that he could see no problem with the Mormons. "Whatever may have been the disposition of the people called Mormons before our arrival here...they have shown no disposition to resist the law or of hostile intentions. There has been so much prejudice and exaggeration concerned in this matter that I found things entirely different from what I was prepared to expect..."
9. DHC, 3:p. 157.
10. DHC, 3:167.
11. DHC, 3:167. This capitulation to the enemy, of course, came after President Marsh had taken his wife's part in a dispute over milk. Mormon neighbors claimed Sister Marsh had not delivered a pint of milk as rich as promised and asked she make up the slight. Escalation of this trivial matter quite likely had its roots in tensions felt by all the saints in this sector of Missouri at this time.
12. Roberts, 1:473.
13. "Millennial Star," Vol. 26, p. 792.
14. DHC, 3:175.
15. Roberts, 1:479.

16. Roberts, Introduction, DHC III:XLIX.
17. See "In Search of Zion" master's thesis, Collette, p. 179.
18. Lyman, p. 29.
19. Of this prison experience Edward says, "We were confined in a large open room, where the cold northern blast penetrated freely. Our fires were small and our allowance for wood and food was scanty; they gave us not even a blanket to lie upon; our beds were upon the cold floors...the vilest of the vile did guard us and treat us like dogs; yet bore our oppressions without murmuring; but our souls were vexed night and day with their filthy conversation, for they constantly blasphemed God's holy name." See *Biographical Encyclopedia*, "Partridge, Edward" by Susan Easton Black, p. 221.
20. *History of Caldwell County*. See pp. 133-151 for entire report of the Haun's Mill incident.
21. Collette, Appendix Q, pp. 189-90.
22. Roberts, 1:512.
23. Roberts, 1:511-515. See also comments by Parley P. Pratt about actions of the Missouri Legislature, pp. 515-520.
24. Lyman, quoting Eliza, p. 28.
25. Lyman, pp. 30-31. Lyman suggests this final exodus from Missouri separated the wheat from the chaff. He compares Edward to the Apostle Peter, who while displaying moments of weakness, nevertheless emerged a courageous and loyal leader in standing up for truth while all around him peers succumbed to religious persecution.
26. DHC, 3:247.
27. Barrett, *Joseph Smith and the Restoration*, p. 420. This is apparently Barrett's opinion, for logical as it may be, there is no reference listed.
28. Ibid, p. 433.
29. DHC, 3:pp. 250-55.
30. The possible number of dead left behind without ceremony in Far West was a subject of discussion at the Mormon History Symposium, Session One, Omaha, NB, May, 1997.

chapter seven

Tragedy and Triumph

As Bishop Partridge gathered his family across the Mississippi River into Illinois, church organization lie in shambles. Many of the leaders, including Joseph and Hyrum, languished in the Liberty Jail, with directions they be shot. Only Gen. Doniphan's courage prevented it when he refused to follow orders from Gen. David Lucas. With this insubordination (for which Doniphan was never punished), Doniphan uttered one of the most revered statements by any non-Mormon in the annals of LDS history: "It is cold-blooded murder. I will not obey your order...if you execute these men, I will hold you responsible before an earthly tribunal, so help me God."[1]

During Joseph's period of incarceration, both friends and enemies visited the prophet, some to encourage him, others to berate him for the loss of a brother, relative or loved one. A few went so far as to blame Joseph for sending loved ones to their cruel reception in Missouri.[2]

Indeed, many of the saints, including Edward, must have pondered at one time or another how different their lives might have been had they been allowed to move directly to Illinois from Ohio. What had going to Missouri gained any of them anyway other than heartbreak...empty attempt for redress ignored by people in high places? If Joseph could not have halted the onslaught, could he not, with his powers of prophecy, at least have foreseen the futility of endless court petitions and the final result: expulsion without the slightest remuneration? Or was it necessary, somehow, for a later judgment in Heaven, that every legal recourse be attempted in a state where judicial process was to prove nothing more than a farce?

In the final routing of Far West, church leaders witnessed

outrages even worse than those in Jackson County. "The mob was now loose upon the unarmed citizens of Far West and under the pretext of searching for arms, they wantonly destroyed much property and shot down cattle just for the sport of it. The people were robbed of their most valuable property, insulted and whipped; but this was not the worst. The chastity of a number of women were defiled by force; some of them were strapped to benches and repeatedly ravished by brutes [Hyrum Smith put the number at 16] in human form until they died from the effects of this treatment."[3]

Why would the Lord send his children to reside among such a degraded and barbaric people...and label it...Zion?

Did the saints, indeed "pollute their inheritance," as warned in the Doctrine and Covenants 103:14 i. e. sin so greatly they did not deserve occupation of the "Promised Land"? Try telling that to Edward Partridge, he who had so meekly, for the sake of Christ, borne the outrage of a lawless mob tearing him from his family in Jackson County.

But to endure, as Edward and Lydia did, along with their children, one must put forth faith, not fear and finger-pointing. There was always the example of the Savior. He could scarcely have been sent among a more savage people at that time than the Romans...and who would argue that the Jewish nation clamoring for His crucifixion was more humane?

When Joseph and the others were finally allowed to escape from the Liberty Jail,[4] the church began to take on signs of earthly composure once again. Joseph's conviction that the malarial swamps in a place called Commerce could be rendered habitable was beginning to reach fruition. Indeed, the saints must have taken heart as Nauvoo blossomed, converts arriving almost daily to build up the "New Zion." Growth was so rapid that by the fall of 1839, the church needed three bishops. Edward was called to be bishop of the Upper Ward, while Brothers Newell Whitney and Vinson Knight officiated the Middle and Lower wards. The members felt organized and unified once again. Things were finally the way they were supposed to be.

Toward the end of 1839, Edward was voted by the local high council to write an article in the "Times and Seasons" instructing brethren to the west not to settle in Kirtland. The church was to gather to Nauvoo. Those who disobediently went to Kirtland were to be disfellowshipped.[5]

It is most likely that Edward was asked to issue this sensitive message because of his reputation for firmness accompanied by sensitivity and tact.

Within a year of arriving in Nauvoo, Emily writes in her journal that the family began to enjoy "happy times."[6] The Lord's silo had been sifted, the chaff sorted out, the wheat only remaining. So it would appear on the surface. Those who had been valiant, including the entire Partridge family, could yet be counted loyal church members. Was this the Lord's "hidden "agenda" all along, as suggested by historian Scott Partridge (a descendent of Edward's) that Missouri's crucible of fire was meant primarily to weed out the weak?[7]

Indeed, some reward was now reaped for the remaining faithful. Immediate fear of mobs was gone,[8] families again resided in social units, church leaders directed ecclesiastical affairs, the saints dared envision permanent homes.

Ironically, during this period of relative tranquility near the swamps of Commerce, Edward grew sick and became bedridden with what was probably malaria. It was likely the first time in years that Bishop Partridge dared let down, no longer on guard to preserve the lives of his family and himself. Like the skipper of a sinking ship, he remained in Missouri as long as he dared. In any event, he soon became too physically weak to carry out his work load in helping the family build a new home. Within weeks, despite the pleading and prayers of family, Edward died.

How could this be...the life of one who had suffered so much now snuffed out with peace and rest within his grasp? How could such an indomitable will be suddenly silenced? Family members must have wondered how one they so depended on could be taken away.

Bishop Partridge was apparently buried somewhere in Nauvoo's old Pioneer Cemetery. A marker was likely put in place, but probably destroyed by church enemies at the exodus several years later. Sadly, through a century and a half, no marker graced the earthly remains of the church's first bishop. As late as summer 1994, this writer could find no official earthly trace that Edward

Partridge ever lived, nor could LDS residents of Nauvoo in early 1997.[9] Questions were asked by family members of church hierarchy why this was so. The oversight was finally rectified Aug. 30, 1997 following family appeals for a proper memorial.[10]

In memorial services, in 1997, it was pointed out that Edward was finally receiving his due for a lifetime of devoted church work. A street in Nauvoo is named after Bishop Partridge. LDS Second Counselor President James E. Faust said that Edward Partridge was a "man of intelligence and character," dedicating the marker to "a remembrance of the life, the example, the faith and the dedication of thy servant Edward Partridge...may it stand as a reminder of the nobility of this great man, his wife and children..."

Bishop H. David Burton added these remarks: "...that great bishop has had his season of rest. I suspect he is very proud of that great faithful posterity you represent." Many Partridge family members were present. The services were conducted by Matthew J. Lyman, great, great grandson of Edward.

The services emphasized that the first bishop had done as so many Latter-day Saints strive to do: he had endured to the end. On the marker were these words: "Born 27 Aug., Died in Nauvoo, 27 May, 1840, D&C 41:9, 11, "I have called my servant Edward Partridge...a bishop unto the church...and this because his heart is pure before me, for he is like Nathanael of old, in whom there is no guile."

Following Edward's death, Joseph Smith penned these words in his History of the Church dated May 27, 1840: "Bishop Edward Partridge died at Nauvoo, age forty-six years. He lost his life in consequence of the Missouri persecutions, and he is one of that number whose blood will be required at their hands."[11] Joseph also noted with sadness that Edward's daughter, Harriet, died eleven days earlier on the 16th.

No doubt, Harriet Pamelia's death had further worsened Edward's condition. Little was apparently said by Edward in his last days. Nothing was recorded. But his obituary which ran in the "Times and Seasons" Vol. I, No. 8 says much about this first bishop of the church:

"Died in this place on the 27th of May, Bishop Edward Partridge, aged 46 years. In recording the death of this our brother, we record the death of one of our earliest, most faithful and confidential members. His life was one continual exhibition of his sincerity of his religious belief and a perpetual evidence of his confidence in a future state of rewards and punishment in view of which he always acted. His strict regard through life, to all commandments of Heaven, and his undeviating obedience to them, are consoling evidence to his friends...[of a life hereafter].

"No man had the confidence of the church more than he. His station was highly responsible; large quantities of money ever entrusted to his care...for the benefit of the poor...driven from his home, found himself reduced to a very limited circumstance, still not one cent of public property would he use to indemnify himself or his family; but distributed it all for the benefit of the widow, the fatherless, and the afflicted; has deceased leaving his family in very ordinary circumstances.

"Had there been one covetous desire in his heart, no man had the opportunity better to gratify it; but he left a testimony, to be had in everlasting remembrance, that he lived above its influence, and over him it had no control but in all things, he had respect to the reward of the just.

"A life of greater devotedness to the cause of truth, we presume, was never spent on his earth. His religion was his all, for this he spent his life, and for this life, he laid it down. He lost his life in consequence of the Missouri persecutions, and he is one of that number whose blood will be required at their hands. As a church we deplore our losses, but we rejoice in his gain. He rests where his persecutors can assail him no more."

The saints also thought highly of Harriet Pamelia: "She was...kind and affectionate to her friends...especially her parents," said the "Times and Seasons" obituary. "She was firm in the everlasting covenant. As a member of the church she was faithful, ever ready to minister comfort and consolation to those around her...in her death, her parents have been deprived of the society of one who was near and dear to them. Blessed are those who die in the Lord."

To objectively evaluate Edward's life, it must be said that he did not escape some chastening from the Lord, as witness D&C

50:39. After emphasizing that no man should hinder them [church leaders] from doing what they have been appointed to do, the verse says, "Wherefore, in this thing my servant Edward Partridge is not justified; nevertheless let him repent and he shall be forgiven." Apparently, the bishop went ahead and tried to resolve problems in Missouri via his own understanding. The next verse cautions all the saints that "they are children and must learn to grow in grace and knowledge of the truth." That, Edward seemed willing to do.

It is true that Edward did not always sheep-like, obey higher directive, especially in the early Missouri period. Historian Collette suggests that Edward disagreed strongly with the prophet on one issue, perhaps failing to provide aggressive leadership when needed. "He so provoked the prophet that he wrote a letter severely rebuking the Bishop...one of the sharpest chastisements in Mormon literature."[12] Excerpts are carried in D&C 85:7-8 as follows, referring to Bishop Partridge, according to Collette: "And it shall come to pass that I, the Lord God, will send one mighty and strong...to set in order the house of God and to arrange by lot the inheritance of the saints...while that man, who was called of God and appointed, that put forth his hand to steady the ark of God, shall fall by the shaft of death, like as a tree that is smitten by the vivid shaft of lightning."

Poetic language and a strong rebuke. It does appear to be directed toward Edward, since he was called to "arrange the inheritances of the saints." But if exasperated with Edward's failure to make the Law of Consecration work in "Zion," in 1834, Joseph must have felt differently in 1838 (at height of the Missouri persecutions) for it was then that he wrote Edward was "one of the Lord's great men...a pattern of piety, without guile as was Nathanael of old."[13]

A similar revelation in D&C 103:16 speaks of a Moses being sent to lead the saints in the redemption of Zion. Edward Jr. was to later say that the Prophet Joseph told him at the funeral of Bishop Partridge (Edward Jr. was then about 7 years old) that "his father was that man, the Moses that was spoken of." Historian S. H. Partridge repeats this idea some 100 years later. But there is no corroboration of the same in Joseph Smith's or other histories written during the Missouri-Nauvoo period. As Collette puts it, there was much speculation as to who this one "mighty and strong," might be. Many have made the claim for themselves or an ancestor. But for now, it will have to remain mere speculation, for there is no way to pinpoint this modern day "Moses." Some church members might say it was Brigham Young, who led the saints to their Zion in the mountains, as did the Israelite leader out of Egypt.

Historian Sidney Sperry says Bishop Partridge had a "stubborn streak in him...it was the practical bent of the man..."[14] He did not always do as instructed by ecclesiastical superiors. At one point Edward asked for forgiveness if he had offended the prophet.[15]

It must also be said that Bishop Partridge lived during particularly difficult times. Church leaders were often a thousand miles away when local matters went awry and decisions had to be made quickly without direct guidance. What if a member refused to deal honestly in the Law of Consecration? How harsh should the bishop be with him? There was the reference in the New Testament of Ananias and Sapphira being struck dead on the spot for holding back in consecrating their goods to the poor, then lying about it.[16] The event caused all who heard of it to fear greatly. It must have seemed to Edward that such an event might help expedite the work in modern times. At least, the members would pitch in more willingly.

Bishop Partridge may well have taken the attitude that he need not be "commanded in all things," long considered a reprimand in LDS Church scripture and philosophy. Then, too, instructions in the D&C (first labeled a "Book of Commandments for Government of the Church") were not compiled until 1833, following many of the calamities in Jackson County. Revelations received after that time were not immediately received by members in Missouri, a thousand miles from Kirtland's church headquarters.

But to measure the man against his peers, let us look at other church leaders of the time and what became of them. Sidney Rigdon, who joined the church about the same time as Edward Partridge and went with him to see the prophet, would soon after Edward's death lose his zeal for the work, seek to be equal to Joseph as a "guardian" of the church, and refuse instruction. After much patience on the part of church leaders, Rigdon, once the prophet's right hand man, was excommunicated.[17] By the end of or shortly after the Missouri expulsion, Joseph had lost both counselors to apostasy or excommunication, seven members of the Twelve, and the entire Far West presidency. Bishop Partridge also lost a counselor. Perhaps this was the reason H. S. Partridge remarked that a faithful Edward "did the best he could under the circumstances."[18]

Keeping one's testimony burning brightly required seeing beyond immediate suffering. One must have the faith to visualize spiritual reward, whether in this life or the next. It would appear that Edward managed to do this in looking beyond immediate suffering.

In modern times, James E. Faust, counselor to LDS President Gordon B. Hinckley, has this to say about his great, great grandfather, Edward Partridge: "[He] was so tortured and humiliated and suffered so much in his calling from lawless mobs that he could not possibly have doubted the genuineness of the revelation that appointed him...he knew Joseph's heart and soul. Grandfather could not have been deceived."[19]

That describes Edward rather well. He knew Joseph's heart and soul, remaining trustworthy to the principles he and Joseph both espoused, even though not always agreeing on policy and procedure. It would appear that Edward knew the heart and soul of the savior well, for like many saints, Edward would need the same to bear so many of his hardships in His name.

As Emily put it in her journal: "There is nothing in this life too dear to sacrifice for the hope that our religion gives us."[20] And this: "When I look back and consider the great responsibility resting upon my father as bishop — his poverty and privations and hardships he had to endure, the accusations of false brethren, the grumbling of the poor, and the persecutions of our enemies, I do not wonder at his early death."

At the same time, the Partridge girls had their immature foibles as would any lacking experience in life. Emily writes in her journal about wishing her parents had given her better clothing to wear. In one act of rebellion against her mother, Emily was sent to repair a hole in her blue dress and did so with a huge white patch. "She felt badly plagued because of her dress."[21] Good clothes or no, of course, all must go to church on Sunday with whatever could be found in a rather poor household. It is quite possible that Edward's desire to avoid appearing better off than others, as keeper of the church's finances, was a fault as well as a virtue...at least in the eyes of his female offspring.

But it would seem that the greatest accomplishment of Edward Partridge was the strength to meet adversity with courage and faith. It was a legacy, exemplified by teaching and example in many powerful ways, he left to church members, as well as his family. This was true in both Nauvoo and the trek west, which family members would make with "faith in every footstep."[22]

It is not likely they could have done this without the strong leadership of their father and husband, who kept his head high and his name clear in allowing no murmuring nor dissent against the Restored Gospel, nor its dedicated leaders.

Eliza's emerging strength, as the eldest Partridge girl, is shown during the dark Missouri period in what must have been inspired by her parents' dogged faith: "We know not what we shall be called to pass through before Zion is delivered and established; therefore, we have great need to live near to God and always be in strict obedience to all of his commandments."

Within two years after Edward's death, two of his daughters tell of maintaining faith through particularly trying times. But much of the affliction was from within, not without. Eliza gives us insight into the devious life of John C. Bennett, who wrangled himself into the confidence of many in Nauvoo, including the prophet. Eliza says that after a falling out with Joseph, Bennett plotted to take Joseph's life while the latter rode horseback on the military parade field, scheming to make it look like an accident. "But the Lord warned Joseph and he was on guard." Joseph does not elaborate in his Church History except to say that Bennett was among a number of "wicked and corrupt men," including former counselor William Law, who sought to take the prophet's life. Both were excommunicated.[23]

Some insights into the trying times in Nauvoo were more personal. Eliza recorded in her journal that after Edward died, she and sister, Emily, went to live in the home of Joseph and Emma for three years. Other members of the family lived for a few weeks with William Law until their home was completed. Law was described by Eliza as "very kind" to the Partridges[24] despite the assertion mentioned above that he conspired to take the prophet's life.

On March 4, 1843,[25] according to Emily's journals, she and sister Eliza entered into the new and everlasting covenant of marriage with Joseph, the ceremony performed by Heber C. Kimball, with witnesses present. Emily would then have been 19, Eliza, 23.

Emily says that Emma not only approved the marriages but "chose my sister and I." "We were sealed in her [Emma's] presence with her full and free consent." But before nightfall, according to Emily's journal, Emma would not allow Joseph to live with either wife long enough to consummate the marriage. "Emma said some very hard things...or blood should flow."[26]

There is no purpose here in vilifying Emma, for according to Joseph's mother, Emma was a godsend to Joseph and his family, having endured many trials and privations, willing to eat whatever food was available and sleep where her husband must go.[27] Yet, after granting permission for Joseph to marry the two Partridge ladies, it appears she recanted by nightfall.

This was a terrible time for both Eliza and Emily, as they described it, for they considered their marriage vows sacred and intended to live up to them in every way as devoted polygamous wives. Joseph, Emily and Eliza soon met with Emma to resolve the crisis. "The understanding was that all was ended between us. I [now] meant to keep the promise I was forced to make." Thus, the sisters must no longer, in practice, consider themselves Joseph's wives, despite the fact documents existed to say they were legally married before man and God. Joseph apparently felt it necessary to keep this arrangement to appease Emma. The matter was not to be discussed further, in or out of the Smith household. Apparently, because the church had so many enemies, ready to persecute for any principle not in mainstream society, polygamy had not yet been announced to the world or even made public within the church.[28]

The two had withstood much travail in their lives but nothing like this. In their agreement with Emma, they not only were not allowed to consummate their marriage with Joseph, but were to not even allow their marriage vows to the prophet be known among general church membership. Emily describes the ordeal this way. "We looked upon the covenants we made as sacred. She [Emma] gave two other wives [Sarah and Maria Laurence) to him [Joseph] and they lived in his house as his wives...but my sister and I were cast off."

Why Emma should allow the other two to live as Joseph's

wives and not the Partridge wives is not known. This statement about the Partridge and Laurence wives directly refutes, of course, the claim made by ministers of the Reorganized LDS Church that Joseph entered into no polygamous marriages. (It is a claim this author has heard more than once from RLDS pulpits.)

The tragedy became deeper for Emily and Eliza the next year, according to both Partridge journals, when Joseph was martyred and they could not even openly mourn for him as his wives. "I went with the rest [to the funeral] as a stranger, none suspecting the extra sorrow that was in my heart," says Emily. Emily says she visited Emma after the funeral and "she was very gracious, for there was no Joseph to be jealous of then." Emily seemed to bear no grudge against Joseph for keeping peace in his household as he did, but wrote in 1883 about Emma: "After these many years I can truly say, poor Emma. She could not stand polygamy. I hope the Lord will be merciful to her. Let the Lord be the judge."

Emily was throughout her lifetime to stand firmly for the principle of polygamy, writing in her diary in later years that she did not feel pity for George Reynolds, doing time in prison (late 1800s) for polygamy. "I pity for the ignorance of our opponents." Since many of them then lived in Salt Lake City, Emily added, "Let our enemies do as we did, go somewhere that is uninhabited. We do not need them."[29]

Quite obviously, Emily was an outspoken individual as a young lady and later as an aging woman. But it was her feistiness and attention to details in her life which make her unpublished journals so valuable in gaining insight into how it was for some in the early church period.

Despite her daughter's trials, mother Lydia was to later say: "Polygamy is true and is an institution of Heaven. I received it from the mouth of the Prophet who taught and practiced it to the day of his death. My children are all in it and they prefer it to monogamy, and their children are as much respected as they otherwise could be, notwithstanding all that our enemies say to the contrary."[30]

This included knowledge on Lydia's part that after the death of Joseph, Emily married Brigham and in his position of church president (leading the exodus west) had precious little time to devote to Emily's personal problems, nor that of any one individual. At least Emily would have strong support from a close and loving family in whatever lie ahead even if her husband was not with her much of the time.

Possibly influencing Emily in marrying Brigham was an item in her diary in August of 1844 in which she stated that she was a witness, among testimonies of other members, that when speaking to the saints, Brigham stood out clearly as the "Lord's choice" to be next president of the church. He seemed to be "transfigured," i.e. take on the appearance of Joseph Smith, his voice and demeanor resembling that of the slain prophet. The attempt of Sidney Rigdon to be a "guardian" for the church was a shallow one alongside that of the president of the Quorum of the Twelve, he who had remained steadfast in the church despite its deep travail while Sidney traipsed off to Pittsburgh.

It appeared important to Emily, as with her sisters, that they marry someone who could lead them spiritually. Being 43 to Emily's 21, Brigham could also play a father's role in her behalf. Edward had been 46 when he died, at a time when his daughters might have leaned on him for much-needed support while blooming into womanhood. Brigham could also help her better understand the gospel amid so many traumatic events in the new church she might have struggled to understand, some past, some surely to come. She would, with her husband, carry out a major role in fulfilling the destiny God planned for His people wherever they were to go.

Eliza and Caroline, who married Amasa M. Lyman at the time he was counselor to Joseph, would not share their husband's spiritual counsel as would Emily. Lyman would, after serving several missions and settling in Utah, abandon his testimony of the Restored Gospel and thus, in effect, spiritually abandon two faithful daughters of Edward and Lydia Partridge.

Yet, it is in the exodus to the Rocky Mountains that we shall discover many more examples of Edward's influence and example, indeed of the rich legacy he left family and friends.

end notes, chapter seven

1. *History of Caldwell County*, p. 137. *Documentary History of Church*, 3:190-191; also see footnote.
2. Letters of Alexander McRae to the weekly *Deseret News*, Nov. 2, 9, 1854.
3. *Documentary History of Church* 3:422. See also Affidavits of Hyrum Smith, p. 422; Brigham Young, p. 434; Sidney Rigdon, p. 464.
4. For further details, see DHC 3:320-21.
5. Ibid, 3:39.
6. A theme of Emily's diaries during the early Nauvoo period. For some reason, perhaps because persecution was so keen in Missouri, none of the Partridge girls recorded their thoughts as frequently as in Nauvoo. Their sporadic writings prior to the Nauvoo period are labeled journals.
7. S. H. Partridge's unpublished manuscript, p. 138, microfilm, LDS Church Archives, SLC, UT.
8. There was yet, however, some threat of Missouri mob action. Officials from that state still seemed incensed that Joseph and Hyrum had escaped jail and sought to extradite them. Some of the mob actually crossed over into Illinois to kidnap several Mormons not even charged with anything in Missouri. See George Q. Cannon, *Life of Joseph Smith the Prophet*, p. 335.
9. Carol Egbert, Layton, UT, is in receipt of a letter from Edithe Finlinson, Nauvoo, IL, dated Feb. 28, 1997, which reads: "We have checked the Visitor's Center Library [LDS] and Lands and Records Office...they tell us that the exact location of his burial site is unknown, just that it is thought to be in the Old Pioneer Cemetery about two miles east on Parleys Street. We have been there several times, walking through the few remaining, badly weathered markers and there is nothing indicating any Partridge graves."
10. The LDS "Church News" of Sept. 6, 1997, page 3, reads in part: "...President James E. Faust visited Nauvoo on Aug. 30 to dedicate a monument at the Old Pioneer Cemetery memorializing Edward Partridge, first bishop of the Church...the marker was made possible by family members who now number in the thousands...no record has been found as to the exact location of his gravesite. However, President Gordon B. Hinckley designated an appropriate location in the Old Cemetery."

    The program included a rendition of Edward's "Let Zion in her Beauty Rise," LDS Hymn Book, P. 41, by the Young Performing Missionaries.

    In a letter dated Oct. 16, 1997, Matthew Lyman, Edward Partridge descendant, reported that some 500 family members, among an estimated 3,000 descendants, donated $11,000 for the memorial. The cemetery site in the program is listed as "Old Nauvoo Burial Ground."

11. DHC, 3:132. Brigham Young was to later say of him, "...Brother Partridge, yes and every other good saint are just as busy in the spirit world as you and I are here." Journal of Discourses, p. 579.
12. D. Brent Collette, "In Search of Zion," master's thesis, Brigham Young University History Department, p. 54. Herein, Collette says Ezra Booth used the differences between Joseph and Edward as an "excuse" for his apostasy. See also footnote 25 on the same page.
13. DHC, 1:128; (Lord speaking, D&C 41:11.)
14. Quoted by S. H. Partridge, p. 133, unpublished, LDS Church Archives, Salt Lake City, UT.
15. Edward was told he had insulted the prophet. See S. H. Partridge, p. 114.
16. Acts 5:1-10.
17. DHC, 7:268. Sidney had gained great favor with the prophet but in the end, he lacked the humility and inner resolve to remain steadfast in an unpopular cause.
18. H. S. Partridge, p. 134.
19. *The Prophet and his Work*, quoting President James E. Faust, 1996.
20. Emily's unpublished diary, among various titles including, "Incidents in the Life of a Mormon Girl," p. 4. Other titles: "Diary of a Mormon Girl, "What I Remember," LDS Church Archives, Salt Lake City, UT. Excerpts are compiled by Albert R. Lyman under the unpublished title of "The Partridge Family Journal."
21. "Partridge Family News Bulletin," August, 1957, Vol. 7, p. 1. The original or primary source of this quote is not given.
22. This was the motto of those who re-enacted the pioneer wagon train journey from Winter Quarters, Nebraska to Salt Lake Valley, in the sesqui-centennial commemoration of 1997.
23. DHC, 7:56-57.
24. Eliza's unpublished journal, unnumbered pages. Reiterated in Partridge Family News Bulletin, August., 1957, p. 4.
25. An early entry in Emily's unpublished diary, this date is given as March 1, 1843 in some Partridge family annals. (See LDS Church Archives, Access no. 3887. Many pages are unnumbered.)

    Some have interpreted the following, recorded by Joseph in his History of the Church 6:46, as saying there was no church-sanctioned polygamy, even as late as October, 1843: "Gave instructions to try those persons who were preaching, teaching, or practicing the doctrine of plural wives; for according to the law, I hold the keys of this power in the last days...and I have constantly said no man shall have but one wife at a time, unless the Lord direct otherwise."

    Also see Scott Faulring, *An American Prophet's Record*, p. 417, wherein Joseph says he "forbids" the practice of polygamy.

But there is also this to consider: according to DHC 6:510, Joseph wrote on July 16, 1843 on the "everlasting covenant" to the effect that a man and wife "must enter that covenant in the world or he will have no claim on her in the next world. *But on account of the unbelief of the people, I cannot reveal the fulness of these things at present* (author's italics). Whether that covenant mentioned was marriage for time and eternity with one wife or more than one was at that time not fully explained. It is unlikely Emily married Joseph at a later date because she talks of his martyrdom as *a year later* (author's italics), June 27, 1844. There seems to be no dispute, however, that Joseph married the two Partridge ladies whatever the precise date. Emily names Heber C. Kimball as a witness to the marriage of herself and Eliza to Joseph. The same is mentioned by Wilford Woodruff in his Discourses, Vol. 23, p. 131.

26. Ibid. It should also be noted that Emma showed signs of severe distress on or about this time in many ways. She begged for Joseph to return from Iowa, where he would in 1844 be safe from enemies, even though Joseph said to do so would be like "going as a lamb to the slaughter." After his death, history records that Emma married a "gentile" unaffiliated with any church and chose not to make the difficult trek west with other church stalwarts.
27. *History of Joseph Smith* by Lucy Mack Smith, pp. 190-91.
28. See DHC, 5:510. Also, preface to D&C 132.
29. Emily's diary, 1874.
30. This comment made late in Lydia's life was copied for posterity by Edward Jr. in the latter of his nine diaries. Pages are numbered but sometimes obscure. See "Sources Cited."

chapter eight

The Legacy

"I took my infant and crossed the river, and was again houseless and homeless in the cold and inclement weather of 1846. I wandered from fire to fire...looking for someone I knew. The day after the crossing, I might be seen sitting on a log in a blinding snowstorm with a three months' old babe in my arms. I will not attempt to describe my feelings at this time but cold and hungry I surely was, and the prospects looked rather dismal."[1]

Thus begins Emily's diary as she makes the Mormon exodus from Nauvoo. She had by now remarried, this time to Brigham Young, one of several wives of the new church president. The Mormon leader was spread so thin looking after the body of the church he now governed that he could scarcely accompany any one individual soul to safety. He would find Emily later as best he could. For now she was on her own.

Even at that she was better off with the infant she named Edward Partridge Young than nine other women who gave birth that first night in Sugar Creek, nine miles west of the Mississippi. It was still a frightening experience, however, for a 22-year old first-time mother with no husband near to help.

Eliza, traveling with sister Caroline (their husband Amasa Mason Lyman helping other saints),[2] wrote that she crossed the Mississippi on ice that was "very dangerous." She says she was very cold and uncomfortable but didn't complain because, "We were leaving the land of our enemies and hoped for better times." As diaries attest, rain and mud and cold slogged their every step and frequently kept sleep at abeyance through the night. Mud and rain hindered travel so severely on some days that no progress west was made at all. Survival was the only immediate focus.

The story of the exodus from Nauvoo in February, 1846 across the partially frozen Mississippi is well known to LDS church members and need not be repeated here. For Emily and others, the reality was that mobs howled from the Illinois shore. Looters roamed the streets of Nauvoo, pilfering anything of value, particularly weapons to wreak further mayhem against saints remaining behind. There was no turning back for any of the Partridge family members now that they had identified with the Latter-day Saint bloc. Like the others, they were a hunted and even hated, people. As with the Israelites of old, they wandered into an unknown wildlands, trying to find a Promised Land out there...somewhere, any place of refuge from torment.

There was no welcome mat. Church leaders had written to the territorial governor of Iowa, in vain. The letter sought some sort of official friendly relationship in temporarily crossing Iowa's 324 miles, planting and harvesting wheat, and assurances they might travel in peace. The letter was never answered. (Ironically, after the saints settled for the winter in western Iowa, their population helped the territory gain needed citizenry for statehood.)

Lydia and her children write of no miracles such as quail floundering into camp, as occurred with the Children of Israel and for those saints who fled Nauvoo later, in September, 1846.[3] Never mind; she and her family must continue without any overt sign that God was with them. But why shouldn't He be? Hadn't they given their all for the Restored Gospel?

Edward's offspring would have to rely wholly on the spiritual cause they believed in to sustain them through another day. It was apparent by now, if not in Missouri, that happiness was not in seeking an easy life but in finding the inner strength to meet its adversities.

Students of Nauvoo history will recall that the saints agreed to leave Nauvoo in the spring after gathering provisions and building wagons, planning to depart in mild weather. When their enemies refused to wait, the Partridges faced the brutal cold of February.

Says Emily, "We crossed on the ice, loaded with the wagons...trusting in the Lord for protection and support."[4] She had done the same at times in Missouri. At least the Illinois rabble did not follow, either because the ice appeared too precarious, or mobbers erroneously supposed they had seen the last of Mormonism.

Explorer-pathmarker John C. Fremont had mapped some of the land westward. But his stories of high mountains, wide rivers and savage Indians only added to the risk of travel toward the setting sun. True, Fremont's report to Congress, readily available to church leaders after his exploration west in 1843-44, was quite positive about settlement in Salt Lake Valley. "There is nothing in the climate of this great exterior region, elevated as it is, surrounded and traversed by snowy mountains, to prevent civilized man from making it home."[5]

But Fremont had his detractors, including Jim Bridger. He called Fremont's maps crude and inaccurate, Fremont's knowledge of the region sketchy. Bridger, of course, was to later tell Brigham that he would give $1,000 (*Journal of Discourses*, p. 736) for the first ear of corn grown in Great Salt Lake Valley. What it amounted to was that the West, and particularly the Rocky Mountains, were at best, roughly charted. Brigham even had a map in his possession from one Augustus Mitchell called "New Map of Texas, Oregon and California" which did not always agree with Fremont's geography.[6] As for Nebraska, there was a spider web of trails across the sandhills, so many that none appeared best. When they did arrive in Nebraska, the pioneers found water so scarce they must try to remain within sight of the winding Platte River. Speculation beforehand could also play grim tricks on the mind. Which routes spoken of would avoid conflict with gentiles?

The Lewis and Clark Expedition of 1804, of course, skirted far to the north and did not attempt to explain what one might expect south of what is now northern Wyoming.

Emily describes her perception of what lay ahead this way: "I faced a wilderness full of wild Indians and wild beasts before me, and cruel, heartless beings behind me..." The possibility of problems with natives had been very real since 1831 when the federal government forced most of the Sauk and Fox tribes from Illinois into Iowa. As late even as 1857, Sioux Indians killed 32 settlers in western Iowa, not far from where the Mormon pioneers trekked toward Winter Quarters.[7]

Before departing Nauvoo, Mother Lydia had married a second

husband, William Huntington, a staunch church member who was appointed a president of one group of saints at Mt. Pisgah, Iowa. Eliza wrote that Father Huntington was "a very good man and very good and kind to mother and her children."

But he soon succumbed to the elements. Emily, the most articulate and succinct writer of the Partridge girls, and by now somewhat hardened by the realities of life, pulled no punches in writing of the event: "The privations and exposures of the journey were too much for Father Hungtington. He soon broke down and lay a corpse." William was buried at Mt. Pisgah.

Thus, barely remarried, Lydia was a widow once more. The Partridge women would cross the plains without a man's day-to-day assistance. As Emily put it, "We had no [adult] male friend left." Edward Jr. was 13 at this time and of some physical help, but still very dependent upon the women for direction and guidance.

For some reason, modern saints suppose upon hearing "pioneer stories" 'that these people were inured to the times, possessing experience equal to their ordeals, more ready for physical challenge than city folks today. That might be true; but one only need read Emily's diary to see that the frontier experience, heading to an unknown destiny in the West, was as frightening to them then as if we today were to find our way across Outer Mongolia.

Writes Emily, "We could hear wolves…only a blanket kept them from entering the family camp." Diaries indicate most of the family was too sick to feel up to such a challenge. The possibility of hostile strangers entering camp at any time, perhaps enemies from Illinois or Missouri, or even state or federal troops chasing them might occur at any time.[8] Sickness in the harsh elements was more a fact than a fear to many of the saints, including Emily. She would write little of this period, except, "On account of ill health, the journey was most unpleasant…I do not wish to look back on that time."

At Mt. Pisgah, Mother Lydia, Lydia, Emily and Edward Jr. decided to remain for a year, possibly too fatigued and disheartened by William's death to continue, while Caroline and Eliza pushed west once again. The sisters had some help here from their husband, who kept bringing up supplies from the rear while the women pressed ahead. Eliza writes that "Brother Lyman"s instructions would often be to ride ahead and "try to find someone with a fire going."⁹

Eliza writes on April 9, 1846: "Started off the grounds and were obliged to double team before we could get off the camping ground. Commenced raining and we were in the midst of a large prairie with no prospect of reaching timber that day and consequently, could have no fire...continued raining very hard...best of teams cannot move their loads without help...it seemed as if both the teams and the people must perish if they stopped there."

At one time they found saints with a fire but the rains soon put it out. "Brother Lyman came up about dark with one team but the one with our beds and provisions was left on the prairie..." That night, she wrote, as many tried to crowd beneath the one small wagon cover, "I do not know why I did not freeze, for I had no bed and very little clothing..." Then, in a plucky sense of humor, "it must be because there was no room for the frost to get in."

Eliza and Caroline tried to remain in touch with their mother, sisters and brother in the Winter Quarters area but Eliza writes that they were at one time on opposite sides of the river (presumably the Missouri) and tried to shout across to one another across the ice and water. "Caroline crossed the river but not without danger." Eliza gave an indication of the closeness she felt with other family members in penning, "I hope we shall never be separated again until death."¹⁰

There was rejoicing when all of the family joined other saints at Winter Quarters. Here they could remain put for a time and build crude cabins for the coming winter. But with Amasa gone, along with other members of the Twelve as the vanguard to Utah, Eliza and Caroline had to build their cabin if one was going to be built. They did so with more gusto after each rainstorm.

As for the journey across Iowa, today's readers can put aside the notion that the saints traveled as a large, protective body. They straggled west as best they could, in huddled groups, with whatever conveyance they might own. Even when reaching the Missouri River, now the border between Iowa and Nebraska, they lived in scattered settlements, a dozen or so in what is now Council Bluffs, Iowa, others across the river. Those on the west side were able to gather together in one community called Cutler Park; but they were required by the local Indian Agency to relocate.¹¹ They remassed near

Florence, Nebraska in what was to be called Winter Quarters.

Eliza suffered an extra dose of grief. Her first son, Don Carlos, born July 14, died in Winter Quarters at the age of five months. In those days, Amasa was much in demand in the church, and apparently much devoted to duty. After reaching Utah with the vanguard company of General Authorities, he traveled to the Southern States. Bringing converts back with him, all joined Eliza and Caroline on the journey from Winter Quarters to Utah.

Let us digress momentarily here to document a little-known event in LDS Church annals which occurred while Lydia and her family were encamped in Winter Quarters. According to land sale records (yet ensconced in the office of the City Recorder in Independence, Mo.)

Lydia and daughters Eliza, Emily and Caroline returned to Missouri on May 5, 1848, for the express purpose of selling the church temple lot site in Independence. This was done for $300, under the direction of Brigham Young,[12] to one James Pool. A quit claim deed (for property originally registered in the name of Edward Partridge as per Missouri law) was signed by Lydia and her daughters for all 63.4 acres of the temple lot site.

Records show that Pool met the Partridges in Atchison County, Mo., in the northwest corner of the state, just over the state line from Iowa, apparently for the purpose of notarizing the transaction within the state of Missouri. Sale of the deed was recorded in Independence June 16, 1848. Ironically, the city recorder at this time was no other than Samuel Lucas, the ex-general who ordered the execution of Joseph Smith in November, 1838.[13]

There is nothing in the diaries of Lydia and her daughters referring to this incident. Why so? It is quite possible that Brigham Young did not want the world to know the temple site had been vacated in case the church could repurchase the property in the near future. The church also had enemies who might wish to see the prophecies and commandments thwarted regarding building of the Jackson County temple as directed in the Doctrine and Covenants.

But if the saints were commanded by the Lord to build a temple on the Jackson County site, why didn't church leaders hold the property by having someone pay back taxes? It would appear that no

Mormon leader trusted Missouri legal officials sufficiently to keep it for the Mormons, even if complying with every aspect of the law. Afterall, not one single act promised by anyone legally representing the state of Missouri, 1831-39, was consummated in behalf of the Latter-day Saints.[14] Why would Missouri officials bother now?

In any event, records show that Lydia Partridge, "widow of Edward Partridge" signed the papers to sell the same.

At the present time, land deeds in Independence show that the LDS Church, Reorganized LDS Church, and Church of Christ (Hedrekites) own sections of the original 63-plus acres. Granville Hedreck and his religious followers managed on Nov. 8, 1869 to obtain the precise three acres dedicated as the temple lot site at the corner of Walnut and Lexington streets.

Enroute west from Winter Quarters, Eliza had a second son born which she named Platte after the place of his birth. She writes of hanging on to him dearly while crossing streams, the wagon pitching back and forth, the water threatening to inundate those inside. "I hung onto my baby and Caroline hung on to me." After reaching Great Salt Lake Valley, the Partridges found shelter in hastily-built log cabins, the floor dirt (and often mud), the roof leaking. But they were safe here and all could gather into a tight-knit family unit once more rather than being scattered across the prairie.

Emily, her sister Lydia, Mother Lydia, and Edward Jr. did not reach Salt Lake Valley until 1848, a year after the mainstream migration. After arriving there, new tragedy struck for Emily. Her son, Edward, died. She said it was the nearest she ever came to giving up. Another straw would break the camel's back. "But it did not fall."

To say it did not fall, of course, is a subjective statement. It would appear that some of her father's gritty faith had formed a halo, if not over her head, within her mind-set. It was just part of the survival mechanism. The incident was not without precedent with the Partridges.

Eliza tells of struggle in Great Salt Lake Valley. Husband Amasa was in Winter Quarters helping other saints (some were his wives) move west. Thus, Eliza, with sisters Caroline and Lydia, went to work in making the first home in six moves which might be free from enemy attack. She gave thanks to the Lord that her family was preserved in the move to the Rocky Mountains but does not sugar-coat the challenge they faced. "We are now at our journey's end for the present...The country [is] barren and desolate. I do not think our enemies need envy us this locality or ever come here to disturb us."[15]

In April 1849, she wrote about life in what was known as Union Fort in south end of Great Salt Lake Valley. "Moved into a log room. There are eight of us to live in this room...we are glad to get this much of a shelter but it is no shelter when it rains, for the dirt roof lets the water through and the dirt floor gets muddy which makes it anything but pleasant." Afterward, they moved onto their own lots nearer the center of town. Here they pitched tents, although winds sometimes blew them down and on one occasion, Eliza's tent burned to the ground.

On a particularly snowy day, the Partridges went to their mother's cabin in the fort and "found her worse off than we were, for the rain was running through the roof and everything in the house was wet. We took her and her effects up to the wagons, deeming it more prudent to live out of doors than in such a house as this." Apparently, there was more shelter in or under the wagons they had used to travel west.

Diaries describe how scarce food was the first two winters. President Young (Emily's husband) sent the Partridges flour, for "they had a scanty allowance for themselves." Eliza said some of the sisters worked and obtained money to buy flour..."but there was none." Neighbors looked after one another; they shared beef, venison, or whatever someone might obtain. In return for food, Eliza, who had learned much of the tailor's trade in Nauvoo, and her sisters, traded sewing services for food.

At least the family had found shelter here from enemies, if not the elements. But rather than remaining in Salt Lake City, they traveled some 100 miles southward to central Utah, where they made homes in Fillmore and Oak City, approximately 20 miles northwest of Fillmore. By then, daughter Lydia had married Amasa, the third of three sisters married to Apostle Lyman. During much of the time they lived in Salt Lake City, Apostle Lyman was in San Bernardino, California to assist Mormon settlements there.

In time, Amasa went on a mission to England. When he returned, his plural wives saw that a change had come over him. He had come to the decision the savior did not atone for man's sins, moved toward the concept of communicating with the dead through what was then called "spiritualism," attempting to do so through seances.[16] Eventually, he became so estranged from the church that his wives said they "hardly knew him." Weighing against him also might have been a series of failures of the church in his eyes, the fact that his work in California was negated when the saints there were called home to fight Johnston's Army. The Mountain Meadows Massacre in southern Utah, blamed by gentiles on the Mormon hierarchy rather than a few fanatic members, angered citizens in the San Bernardino area. They railed against the Mormons in their midst and prevented their return after the scare of Johnston's Army had abated. There is noting in Lyman's writings, however, to indicate the above had direct effect upon him. His overt differences with the church seemed to be doctrinal.

Living in polygamy must have been a particular trial to the Partridge sisters, even with their husband gone so much of the time. Eliza writes of her experience with plural marriage thusly: "I am often led to wonder how it was a person of my temperament could get along with it and not rebel, for I thought my trials were very severe; but I know it was the Lord who kept me from opposing his plans, although in my heart I felt I could not submit to them. But I did and I am thankful to my Heavenly Father for the care he had over me in those troubled times."

The Partridge women possessed many practical skills, unique even for frontier times. According to historian Emmeline Wells, Emily not only could card, spin, dye, hand-sew with fancy stitching, knit, darn, make soap and candles but excel at all of them." She and her sisters were homemakers *par excellence,* enjoying many insightful ways often referred to as "Yankee ingenuity."[17] They also had their idiosyncrasies and hang-ups. It was written that Emily was willing to discuss with almost anyone in private conversation her hard times in Missouri "but could never be induced to speak in public." She would have had a lot to say, but preferred instead to write in journals for a future posterity. Because she wrote so prolifically, more is known about her than many of the other Partridges.

Not all of her entries were cheerful. "My dear children, I hope you will never know by experience what your parents have suffered." Her diary indicates her greatest joy in life was in passing along to offspring (and her sisters and brother) faith and strength in whatever might sustain them in their own difficulties. Another entry in 1874 at the age of 50: "To look back on my past seems like a troubled dream. The memories are not all pleasant." Also: "I have been associated with this church almost from my earliest recollection and I have been intimately associated with the leaders of this people and I know they are good men, and I can testify of their worth. They are very far from being the bad characters their enemies represent them, and I will say a word for the women. I think there are some of the best women in this church the world affords. A gentile woman was stopping with me a short time and she said the best women she ever saw were among the Mormons."[18]

Emily, who died in 1899, might have possibly read the *History of Caldwell and Livingston counties* published in 1886 in St. Louis. Yes or no, she knew what persecution her family had been through due to theological discrimination. Today's Latter-day Saints know little about how massive this discrimination was. For example, in the preface of *History*, the writers and editors say: "From the most authentic official and private sources...publication has been long delayed that it be an accurate history..." Then the book solemnly states, "Nothing in the history of fanaticism equals the progress of Mormonism...that an uneducated youth without...common morality (for the founder of Mormonism is said to have been a dissolute, unprincipled young rake and notorious for his general wickedness) could operate on the public credulity by means of the wildest and most ridiculous pretensions to divinity and prophecy...his followers were to reign and crush the unbelieving world beneath their righteous rule." The same source labels the Book of Mormon, sacred to Latter-day Saints as another witness for Christ, as "blundering, meaningless fiction" and would cause the native Americans "to take over civilized society."

Further, "Joseph Smith had practiced "vicious habits of swearing, swindling and drunkenness... Dreadful stories were told of the conduct of the Mormons...they were charged with being abolitionists."[19]

With these excerpts from the "objective and accurate" history of Caldwell County, it is easier to see the misunderstanding, prejudice and malice which Emily and other members of her family (plus all the saints in Missouri) lived with daily. To avoid holding feelings of anger and revenge years later must have been more than a little difficult. But hadn't their long-suffering and patient father, Edward Sr., set such an example for them?

It should be added that these statements do not necessarily reflect the thinking of all Missourians, particularly in the St. Louis area. Many there, removed from the rough frontier and backwoods element of western Missouri, symphatized with the saints from the beginning, or at least their rights as citizens under the law. In recent times, when LDS President Ezra T. Benson died, it was a front page story in St. Louis newspapers. The LDS temple dedicated in St. Louis in 1997 has been well received by the general population in that region, according to modern newspaper accounts.[20]

As for those Partridge daughters of which little has been said, Caroline and Lydia, much less was known; they did not record their experiences in length. Almost nothing has been preserved about daughter Lydia, but according to historian Lucretia Lyman Ranney, much of what Caroline said was preserved in writing by her children and grandchildren.[21]

All of the Partridge women, faithful to their heritage and membership as taught by their parents, were soon pressed into lengthy church service in their new homes in the Fillmore area. For example, Caroline served as president of the Oak Creek Ward Relief Society for 32 years. On her 79th birthday, she wrote, "...I wonder how many opportunities for doing good to my associates have I neglected. In all the years I have lived, my desires have been to do all the good I could..."[22]

Like Caroline, Eliza showed the spirit of service in moving from an established home in Fillmore to help a grandson. "When she was 59 years of age, her daughter Caroline died after being married only 13 months, leaving a young baby..." Eliza moved with the baby to Leamington [not far north of Oak City] where her daughter-in-law could nurse the baby daily.[23]

Not much is said in the diaries of the Partridge girls about the adversities met by their mother after arriving in Utah. Nor does Lydia say much about it herself. But this was a description of her in the late 1800s: "She lived until she was nearly age 85 and within a few years of her death was busy constantly making quilt blocks, sewing carpet rags, braiding straw and making hats [as did her husband]. She was especially skilled in making buckskin gloves...when they were taking up donations for the Manti Temple, she donated seven pairs of home-made gloves..." The same, not factory made, would have occupied many days of work for Lydia.

Her children said she did many such good works "without boasting," from "a natural kindness of her heart."[24]

The Partridges lived in harmony and peace, it would seem, for several decades in their Millard County homes. They were not the Zion designated for Jackson County, the one Edward lamented losing, but the one wherein it is said, "...for this is Zion — the pure in heart."[25]

For those who might think Mother Lydia lost any faith in the cause she espoused with Edward through her years of suffering since joining the church nearly half a century earlier, she said in 1877: "I have a desire to bear my testimony to the world of the belief I have in the everlasting gospel which is revealed to us in the last days...I have been a member [of this church] over 45 years and have never had cause for a doubt to cross my mind as to the truth of the Latter-day work. I was acquainted with Joseph Smith and believed him to to be a true prophet of God who was willing to lay down his life...I know for myself that the gifts of the gospel are in the church now as anciently. I received not my testimony from man but as the Apostle Peter when Jesus said unto him, 'flesh and blood hath not revealed it unto me but my Father which is in Heaven...' and although man and woman too will set at naught these things, against the truth, yet it will roll forth to the ends of the earth and will prevail over everything that rises in opposition to it, while those who fight against it will be brought to shame and everlasting contempt and will reap the reward for their evil doing."[26]

When Mother Lydia died at Oak City (originally called Oak Creek) in June, 1878, her granddaughter Eliza Maria writes, "We commenced immediately to prepare to take her to Fillmore as she had requested us lay her beside her daughter Lydia who had been buried there over three years. Making a trip of some 20 miles with a body in warm weather was no pleasant task. Eliza laments that even close neighbors declined to help. They "showed us no kindness at all, with the exception of one Brother John Lovell...and one Sister Rebecca Dutson Jacobsen."[27]

Did Eliza's word "kindness" here simply mean lack of direct physical assistance in caring for the body? Afterall, Lydia's daughter Caroline served 32 years as president of the relief society in this frontier community. There is a mention in Oak City histories which say the Partridges were involved in some sort of dispute over irrigation water.[28] But this occurred in 1893, 15 years after Lydia died, and the matter was resolved the very next day.

In any event, the Partridges are much remembered in Oak City today with a reunion in their honor every Memorial Day.[29]

Emily was one of the most outspoken of her sisters on many subjects, or at least it would appear so from what she shared with posterity. She had a strong feeling about corsets. "Every corset in the territory should be cremated, to make way for a healthy circulation of blood."

Eliza possessed, perhaps, the most tactful, insightful, way of sharing her feelings. When husband Amasa began to falter in his testimony of the Restored Gospel, Eliza wrote: "Brother Lyman began to feel uncomfortable in his mind, and I thought many times did not enjoy that portion of the spirit of the Lord that a man in his position should, he being one of the Twelve Apostles. I did not know what was wrong with him, but I could see that he was very unhappy."

This is what Edward Jr. had to say at the funeral of Amasa M. Lyman in Fillmore on Feb. 5, 1877, as he attempted to give the prodigal husband of his three sisters any due he might have coming: "Over 30 wagons and carriages attended, being the largest procession that was ever seen in Fillmore, I believe. The meeting was addressed by John Kelley, an apostate [apparently by previous request by Amasa]. His remarks were very good, considering his principles." The deceased "was dressed in black [rather than temple garments]...a rather pleasant looking corpse. Thus ended the earthly career of a man of more than ordinary ability who spent the greatest part of his life in preaching the doctrines of the Latter-day Saints and finally died a spiritualist. He had many friends and few enemies. A man who always taught and practiced honesty and morality as he understood it."[30]

Edward notes that shortly before Amasa's death, a son, Elder F.M. Lyman, "preached a splendid discourse on the mission of

Jesus," in the presence of his errant father. Amasa had the "privilege of hearing his son advocate the principle that he denounced since his apostasy."

It would appear that the Partridge wives and mothers were so strong in their conviction of the Restored Gospel, and so successful in infusing it into the lives of their children, that Amasa's deviant spirit did not have any persuasive, noticeable impact on any of his progeny.

To show the practicality of his nature, and of the times, Edward's next entry after telling of Amasa's funeral is, "Started with two teams and two hands to [cut] cedars for fence posts." Often after a philosophical discourse, the frontier nature of his life looms in passages such as "skinned a fat hog today."

As shown in his accomplishments, Edward Jr. was forced to grow up in a hurry.

By the time the Partridges moved from Great Salt Valley to central Utah, he was nearing manhood. As a boy, he had witnessed the Christ-like response of his father to persecution in Missouri. Edward Jr. learned about fear and hatred aimed toward an unpopular minority group at an age when most boys today are playing marbles. At 14, he left his family in Great Salt Lake City for a time to go back to Missouri, still potentially enemy territory. No reason was given in family histories, but ostensibly it was to see if material possessions left behind might be recovered. It was man's work and he seemed to be up to it.

At the age of 21, Edward Jr. served a mission to the Sandwich (Hawaiian) Islands and returned some 25 years later to serve there as mission president. He dedicated the LDS chapel at Laie, Hawaii, where the temple now stands.[31]

He was set apart as a bishop in Fillmore, served as high councilor, counselor to stake president A. O. Smoot (in Provo) and after the latter's death, as stake president until his own death in 1900. He also served in many civic capacities, including a judge in Millard County and state legislator.[32] His elected positions show the respect peers had for him.

Following in his father's footsteps, Edward Jr. lived the kind of life which led one historian to say, "He was a quiet, unobtrusive, sensitive man whose whole life has been devoted to the furtherance of the work of God. He was earnest and sincere in all his undertakings and merited and enjoyed the respect of the community...[he] leaves a record without blemish to be cherished and honored by his posterity..."[33]

One of the kindest things said about her parents was by a daughter, Mary Olaha Partridge, who reflected briefly but powerfully on the family's tradition of helping out in the gospel in any manner they could: "...mother used to go out nursing the sick...I had a very happy childhood..."[34]

Edward Jr. married Sarah Lucretia Clayton on Feb. 4, 1858 and took Elizabeth Buxton as a second wife Feb. 15, 1862. All lived in Fillmore for a time, then Sarah in Provo; Elizabeth remained in Fillmore. Homes they lived in, now on the Utah Historical Register (so marked with plaques), show the Partridge's unique penchant for attractive architecture and comfortable details, even in pioneer times.

We have a greater insight into Edward Jr's life via the nine lengthy diaries he kept, numbering more than a thousand pages.[35] He had sometimes lamented that his father did not maintain a more detailed account of his life, and determined not to make that mistake. If we do not know as much about Edward Sr. as we would like, we can discover much about him, or at least his rich legacy he left behind through the life of Edward Jr.

His entries include many philosophical musings. For example, Diary One complains of Ulysses S. Grant being re-elected president. "His administration will do all he can against us...but it matters not who is president as long as the Lord rules and we know he does."

Another entry: "We should not be ashamed to descend as low as our Saviour did." When ordained bishop of Fillmore: "This is something I have always had an instinctive dread of since I have had an understanding sufficient to know what the office of bishop was."

As a probate judge, Edward once faced an interesting case. A young man had dragged Edward's daughter from the dance floor when she chose to be escorted home by someone else. One S. R. Huntsman found that Emily was not one to succumb meekly to bullying. A fight ensued on the dance floor in full view of many others. The young man, arrested for disturbing the peace, was ordered to appear before Emily's father, Judge Partridge. After pleading guilty and appearing contrite, the offender was only fined

$20 and court costs of $8.95. Apparently, the judge, longsuffering like his father, bore no grudge with sinners, even those personally involved with a daughter. His diary does not tell us how Emily felt about it.[36]

An entry which may have relationship to the above: "It has been said that it is better to give than receive. The ability to forgive an injury is evidence of greatness. A narrow, selfish mind is vindictive and revengeful. How much more worthy of our approbation is that mind which is above taking offense at trifles." Also: "Is any man better than a brute who would mistreat a wife or innocent children for the simple reason that he is [physically] strong and they are weak?" Truly, we gain an insight into the soul of Edward Jr. with these thoughts.

After returning as mission president from Hawaii, Edward found that people who owed him up to a thousand dollars or more claimed poverty and could not pay. His observation of one who owed him $200: "He looked comfortably fixed to me." Edward did not pursue the matter, even though as an ex-judge, he obviously knew local law well enough to do so. He wrote in his diary:

> If I do nothing that I will be ashamed to record in this book, it will be well for me. I trust that will be the case.[37]

Edward's last diary entry was May 28, 1899, the year before he died, noting that he presided at the funeral of a friend. His age of 66 is showing at this point, for the rich details usually accompanying such an entry are not there. Edward Jr. was buried in the Provo City Cemetery and unlike the unhappy incident with his father, the grave was well marked at his burial.

These excerpts from Edward Jr.'s diaries are not intended to fully portray the selfless life he lived, but only to indicate the deeply spiritual qualities of the man. His was a legacy exemplified by his father, carried forward by Lydia and her children.

Surely, Bishop Partridge would have been proud of them. His family had lived up to the words of the song he composed in Missouri in the midst of their sorest affliction:

The Legacy

"O may our minds be drawn away
From worldly cares just now
That we may worship thee our God
While at thy feet we bow

O let thy blessings shower around
By day and also night;
Not only us but all thy saints
Who in thy law delight."

end notes, chapter eight

1. Early in Emily's diary. See "Sources Cited" for a description on where to find Emily's diaries in the LDS Church Archives, Salt Lake City, UT.
2. Caroline married Amasa Lyman Sept. 6, 1844. Eliza married Amasa M. Lyman Sept. 25, 1845, five months before the mainstream exodus west. The sisters left Nauvoo Feb. 26, 1846.
3. As described by William Henderson, *Our Mayflower Ancestors and Descendants*, Jocelyn Faux, pp. 419-20, some saints witnessed what truly seemed a miracle: "...we would surely have starved to death had it not been for our kind and Heavenly Father in sending flocks of quail into our camp...some fell into the laps of the women." Henderson said they lived on the quail for three days. Orson Hyde wrote of a similar experience: "...our little children could catch them."
4. Emily also writes during this migration that other church members, aware she was a plural wife, wanted to "look upon the spiritual child" which was hers. It was an indication the practice of polygamy was by now being acknowledged and accepted by many church members. The entries of the trek west are early ones in Emily's diary which she began keeping almost daily shortly before the exodus from Nauvoo.
5. *Narratives of Exploration and Adventure*, John Charles Fremont, p. 258. Fremont also said that he believed the fertile Salt Lake Valley was eminently fitted for settlement. "The bottoms are extensive, water excellent, timber sufficient, the soil good." It was this report, along with others on Oregon and California, which helped send thousands of wagons into the setting sun. Source: Allan Nevins, an editor of Fremont's reports.
6. The original map, located after years of searching, was found reposed in the Brigham Young University Special Collections. The news of how this map was found was a feature of the Mormon History Symposium in Omaha, Nebraska, May, 1997. While the precise importance of this map to the early pioneers in deciding routes west is not known, it is interesting that several maps existed which were not necessarily in agreement with one another.
7. *World Book Encyclopedia*, Vol. I, p. 311-12.
8. Federal troops did, indeed, descend upon the pioneer company at Mt. Pisgah and Winter Quarters, "throwing the saints into great confusion," but it was for the purpose of asking for volunteers to fight the war with Mexico. See DHC 7:612.
9. Eliza's diary, unnumbered pages, LDS Church Archives, typescript and microfilm. See also Lucretia Lyman Ranny, *Our Priceless Heritage*, part II, pp. 11-13.
10. Eliza's diary. See Ranney, Edward Partridge Section, p. 13.

11. The saints' troubles with Indians were not over just because they had reached the Winter Quarters-Council Bluffs (originally called Kanesville) area. One Samuel Henderson Sr. stated that Indians were whooping it up and stealing their livestock. "...One of the Indians came to the door and could not get in, so they shot the cow and went away." *Our Mayflower Ancestors and their Descendants*, p. 420.

12. Recorded in minute form, *Journal History of the Church*, April 26, 1848. The reason given was "to obtain the means to emigrate to the valley." Since the deed was in the name of Edward Partridge's heirs, Lydia was the only one who could sell the temple property.

   See also Discourses of Brigham Young, pp. 181-85, plus Roger Young's *As a Thief in the Night*, listed in "Sources Cited."

13. As an avowed enemy of the Mormons, Lucas most likely welcomed this purchase, supposing it would thwart the LDS prophecy that a temple would be built on the site. Note: today's city records in Independence are stored away in vaults within moisture and insect-limited limestone caves dug out from previous mining operations. Thus, such records dating back more than 150 years are in excellent condition even today.

14. It might certainly be argued that Generals Atchison and Doniphan worked in behalf of the Mormons, but this was in an unofficial capacity. Their efforts were not upheld by those in higher power. Doniphan also succeeded in the Missouri Legislature in getting Caldwell County "set aside" for the Mormons, but when Gov. Boggs later issued the order to exterminate all Mormons, this act was, for all practical purposes, nullified.

15. Eliza's diary entry of Oct. 17, 1848. Of course, Johnston's Army was to come as an enemy nine years later, but as history records, no physical harm came of it.

16. Lyman's unpublished journals, hand-written, are not generally in circulation; but a study of them by historian Davis Bitton includes mention of "seances" during the early 1870s. See also Diary No. Two of Edward Partridge Jr.(Some of the entries, handwritten, are difficult to read.) Brigham Young University Special Collections, Lee Library, Provo, UT.

17. "LDS Women of the Past, Personal Impressions," *Women's Exponent*, Vol. 37, No. 3, October 4, 1908.

18. Emily's diary written in Fillmore. In her latter years, Emily was more prone to philosophize about her past life, perhaps because it required the passing of several decades to put it all in perspective, especially the suffering. She complained less of it with the passing of time.

19. P. 106-125, Caldwell section. But to be fair to the authors of Caldwell County, they do acknowledge that the first schools in Missouri were taught by the Mormons in 1838. Strangely, the authors claim to have received much of their information from Franklin D. Richards, "Mormon historian." It is tragic that such Missouri histories could not have been written as objectively as Flavius Josephus when (although remaining very much a Jew) he summed up Jesus as ... "a wise man..." *Antiquities of the Jews*, Josephus, Ch. XVIII, no. 2, ch. 3. See further explanations in *Life of Joseph Smith* by George Q. Cannon, p. 358.

20. A story in the LDS "Church News" dated June 7, 1997, says, "In the early days, St. Louis was an oasis of tolerance and security for Latter-day Saints...In 1838, the St. Louis Daily Evening Gazette and other newspapers expressed sympathy for the Latter-day Saints and condemned the forces that were persecuting them and trampling their rights. Some citizens held fund-raisers to assist the destitute Latter-day Saints."

In addition, an LDS publication, "Hosanna!" stated at the dedication of the St. Louis Temple in 1997 that more than 220,000 requests had been received for tickets to attend the temple open house.

21. Ranney, Part II, p. 16.
22. Quoted in the *Partridge Family News Bulletin*, August, 1957, Vol. 7, p. 4.
23. From *Echoes of the Sage and Cedars*, a Centennial History of Oak City, UT, p. 391-92 compiled by Margaret W. Roper. Repeated in *E.P. Family Bulletin*, August, 1957, Vol. 7, p. 2.
24. *Edward Partridge Family News Bulletin*, August, 1955, No. 5, from earlier diaries of the children and grandchildren.
25. D&C 97:21.
26. Edward Partridge Jr., Diary Two, entry date Jan. 1, 1877. He said he "copied the following from the pen of my mother." (While she didn't keep a daily diary, later in life she penned many thoughts preserved for posterity by her children.) BYU Special Collections, Lee Library. For further tribute to Lydia's faith and endurance by a Partridge descendent, see Melvin A. Lyman's novel, "Lydia."
27. Copied from the diary of Eliza Maria Partridge Lyman, Sunday, June 9, 1878, according to the *Partridge Family News Bulletin*, August, 1955, No. 8.
28. *Echoes of Sage and Cedar*, p. 134. The text reads from minutes of a town board meeting June 16, 1893 as follows: "It was reported that Partridges had took [sic] out the water of Dry Creek and was wasting it. It was fully concluded to have them stop immediately...or they would be prosecuted." Since this occurred at a place known as the "Partridge Mill," it is not known how much legal right the Partridges of Oak City might have had to divert said water. The problem was, however, rectified June 17 (next day) when water was returned to the main channel. The Partridges had been using the water to "wash out ditches," according to board meeting minutes.
29. This reunion has been hosted annually for many years with a breakfast in Oak City hosted by Partridge descendants Angie Finlinson and Willis J. Lyman (grandchildren of Caroline). Up to 1,000 people have taken advantage of this breakfast, according to a letter received by the author from Finlinson. The family will continue to host the event "until the Millennium," the letter stated.
30. From Edward Jr.'s Diary No. 2. This designation as "spiritualist" is never fully defined by the Partridge family, possibly because they didn't fully understand it themselves. All that was apparent to the wives, according to their journals, is that he lost interest in living the simple and fundamental gospel principles in which the wives abided.
31. For details, see *Unto the Islands of the Sea*, R. Lanier Britsch, particularly p. 139.
32. Ranney, Part II, p. 16.

33. "Biographical Encyclopedia, Partridge, Edward," p. 488, Susan Easton Black.
34. Given in Mary's own words as she reflected on her life as a Partridge. She was a daughter of Elizabeth Buxton Partridge, Edward Jr.'s second (plural) wife.
35. These nine handwritten diaries and journals are in the Brigham Young University Special Collections Section. They commence from May 4, 1854, the year he served a mission in the Hawaiian Islands and continue almost until his death in 1900.
36. Edward Jr., Diary No. Two. Date Dec. 28, 1879.
37. These entries are gleaned from Diaries Five, Six, Seven, spanning the period Jan. 17, 1883 to April 3, 1885.

Sources Cited — Primary

Note: Frequently used book titles are shown abbreviated here as used in End Notes.

Unpublished references written by Edward Partridge:

Journals of 1818 (business), and 1835-37 (missionary travels). Edward's original pocket book journals are in LDS Church History Archives, Salt Lake City, Utah, and have been viewed, in Edward Partridge's own handwriting, by the author. On second reference, these journals are abbreviated EP in End Notes following each chapter.

"Long Journal of Edward Partridge" compiled by Edward Partridge Jr., Fillmore, Utah, 1878, located in LDS Church Archives and among some family members. Includes writings of wife, Lydia, on conversion to Mormonism in 1830, and subsequent events. Includes letters from Edward to wife, to Joseph Smith, to Oliver Cowdery. Copies of affidavits written to Missouri legislature. Letters from Joseph Smith. Hymns. Documents pertaining to life of Edward Sr. For a more complete description of this journal, see historian Davis Bitton's "Guide to Mormon Diaries and Autobiographies," p. 269.

Unpublished references by Lydia Partridge (in addition to above):

Memoirs written late in life at Fillmore, Utah and compiled by family members, including Edward Partridge Jr. and Albert R. Lyman. Located in LDS Archives.

Unpublished references written by children of Edward/Lydia Partridge:

Journals (to 1846) and diaries written by Eliza, Emily, Caroline. Located in LDS Archives. Typescript and microfilm. Most pages are not numbered. Edward Jr., nine-volume diaries, original handwriting, numbered pages, although some in later volumes are not legible. Brigham Young University H. B. Lee Library, Special Collections. Also in possession of Partridge family members.

Note: Eliza's diaries are sometimes listed as "Treasures of Pioneer History."

Emily's journals and diary titles include "Diary and Reminiscences," 1874-1899, "Diary of a Mormon Girl" and "What I Remember." For Emily's journals and diaries, see call # MS 2845. Access No. 3887-Arch-88, LDS Church Library Archives. Note: Bitton refers to Partridge women writings as "journals" prior to l846, and diaries afterward; only then did they contain daily entries. The same labeling format has been followed herein.

Other Primary References Listed Alphabetically

Barrett, Ivan J., *Joseph Smith and the Restoration, History of the Church to 1846*, 1973, Young House, BYU Press. (Original comments and conclusions.)

Bible, Holy, King James translation, *New and Old Testament*

Book of Mormon, LDS Church.

Britsch, R. Lanier, *Unto the Islands of the Sea*, 1986, Deseret Book, Salt Lake City, UT.

Caldwell County, Mo. History, Vol. I, 1985, various authors, Caldwell County Historical Society, Kingston, MO.

Clay County Mo. Sesquicentennial Souvenir, 1972, Alexander Doniphan Daughters of Revolution, Al's Printing Service, Liberty, MO.

Doctrine and Covenants, LDS Church.

Faust, James E., *The Prophet and his Work*, 1996, Deseret Book, Salt Lake City, UT. (Original comments and conclusions.)

Fremont, John C., *Report of the Exploring Expedition to Oregon and California in 1843-44*, Issued by various publishers.

Hickman, W. Z., *History of Jackson County, Mo.*, 1920, Historical Publishing Co., Topeka, Kansas. Reprinted 1990 by Southern Historical Press, Greenville, S. C.

History of Caldwell and Livingston Counties, no author listed, 1886, St. Louis National Historical Society, Nixon-Jones Printing, St. Louis, MO.

Josephus, Flavius, *Antiquities of the Jews*, Book XVIII, Ch. III, p. 379, reprinted 1960, Kregal Publications, Grand Rapids, Mich.

Lyman, Albert R., unpublished typescript and microfilm (comments and conclusions), "Edward Partridge Family Journal," 1954, LDS Church Archives.

Majors, Alexander, *Seventy Years on the Frontier*, edited by Prentiss Ingraham, 1893, Rand McNally, Chicago and New York; reprinted 1985, Allied Publ. Group, Merriam, Kansas.

Partridge, Ruth Louise, *Other Drums*, (fiction) 1974, self-published, Provo, UT.

Partridge, Scott Herald, unpublished manuscript, original thoughts and conclusions, LDS Church Archives, Salt Lake City, UT. Call # MS 14876, access 214441-Arch-96.

Pearl of Great Price, LDS Church.

Pratt, Parley Parker, *Autobiography of PPP*, 1938, Deseret Book, Salt Lake City, UT.

Ranney, Lucretia Lyman, *Our Priceless Heritage*, Parts I, II, (genealogical research), 1959, self-published, Salt Lake City, UT.

Roberts, B. H., *Comprehensive History of the Church of Jesus Christ of Latter-day Saints* (referred to as "Roberts" after first mention; independent research and conclusions), 1930, Deseret News Press, Salt Lake City, UT.

Smith, Joseph Jr., *Documentary History of the Church* (DHC), 1951, Deseret Book, Salt Lake City, UT.

Smith, Lucy Mack, *History of Joseph Smith*, 1979, edited by Preston Nibley, Bookcraft, Salt Lake City, UT.

Wilcox, Pearl, *Jackson County Pioneers*, 1975, Independence, MO., self published.

Wilford Woodruff Journal, compiled by M. F. Cowley, 1909, Deseret News Press, Salt Lake City, UT.

Woodruff, Wilford, Discourses, Volume 23.

Young, Brigham, *Discourses*, 1925, arranged by John A. Widstoe, Deseret Book, Salt Lake City, UT.

Personal Interviews / observations / correspondence

Brown, Larry K., director, LDS Visitors Center, Independence, MO, Oct. 13, 1997.

Hedrekite Church members, temple lot site, Independence, MO, May 29, 1994.

Far West temple lot site, historical displays, May 29, 1994.

Fillmore, UT, home built by Edward Partridge, Jr., 1996.

Fillmore, UT, Territorial Legislature Building and Museum (state park), artifacts and mementoes of Edward Partridge, Jr., 1996.

Fillmore, UT, city cemetery, burial markers for Lydia Partridge, Amasa M. Lyman 1996.

Jones, Lyraine (Former resident of Oak City, UT), June 17, 1997.

Kimball, James, LDS Church Library/Historians Office, Salt Lake City, UT, Sept. 22, 27, Oct. 9, 13, 1997.

LDS Visitors Center, historical displays , Florence, NB, 1996.

LDS Visitors Center, Independence, MO., historical displays, 1994.

LDS Visitors Center, Nauvoo, IL, historical displays. Nauvoo: city cemetery and homesites, 1994.

Mormon History Assn. convention, Omaha, NB, references to presentations about Latter-day Saints buried in Far West, MO; references to trek west from Winter Quarters, Nebr., May, 1997.

Provo, UT, city cemetery, burial marker for Edward Partridge Jr.

RLDS Visitors Center, Independence, MO, historical displays, 1996

Whittaker, David J., curator, 19th Century Western and Mormon Americana, Special Collections and Manuscripts, H. B. Lee Library, Brigham Young University, Provo, UT, Oct. 17, 1997.

Wixom, Mary Aloha Partridge (daughter of Edward Partridge, Jr./Elizabeth Buxton) 1952, interview at her home in Logan, UT. Also, document written about childhood and early married life experiences in moving from Fillmore, UT; copy in author's possession.

Vital documents: (including record of Jackson County Temple Lot sale by Lydia Partridge, 1848) see Appendices. Copy in possession of author.

Sources Cited — Secondary

Listed in alphabetical order:

Bitton, Davis, *Guide to Mormon Diaries and Autobiographies, 1930, BYU Press,* Provo, UT.

Black, Susan Easton, *Biographical Encyclopedia,* LDS Church Library, Salt Lake City, UT.

Hill, Donna, *Joseph Smith, the First Mormon, Doubleday,* Garden City, NY.

Cannon, George. Q., *Life of Joseph Smith, the Prophet,* 1964, Deseret Book, Salt Lake City, UT.

Collette, D. Brent, "In Search of Zion: a Description of early Mormon Millennial Utopianism as Revealed through the Life of Edward Partridge," August, 1977, master's thesis, Brigham, Young University, Provo, UT.

Faux, Jocelyn, *Our Mayflower Ancestors and their Descendants,* 1992, Linrose Publishing Co., Fresno, CA.

Geddes, Joseph, *The United Order among the Mormons,* 1924, Deseret News Press, Salt Lake City, UT.

Jenson, Andrew, *LDS Biographical Encyclopedia,* Vol. I, 1901, originally published by the Jenson History Publishing Co., Salt Lake City, UT.

Jesse, Dean, "Steadfastness and Patient Endurance," unpublished manuscript, Brigham Young University, Provo, UT (see also June 1979 Ensign, LDS Publications).

Ludlow, Daniel H., *A Companion to your study of the Doctrine and Covenants,* Vol II, 1978 Deseret Book, Salt Lake City, UT.

Ludlow, *Encyclopedia of Mormonism* (Edited by), 1992, Macmillian Press, New York, NY.

Lyman, Albert R., "Amasa Mason Lyman, Trailblazer and Pioneer from the Atlantic to the Pacific, Vol. I," 1957, published by Melvin A. Lyman, Delta, UT.

Lyman, Melvin A. *Lydia* (fiction), Old Rugged Cross Press, Roswell, GA, 30075.

McConkie, Bruce R., *Mormon Doctrine,* 1979, Bookcraft, Salt Lake City, UT.

Mullen, Robert, *The Latter-day Saints, The Mormons Yesterday and Today,* 1966, Doubleday and Co., Garden City, NY.

Nibley, Preston, *Brigham Young, the Man and his Work,* 1970, Deseret Book, Salt Lake City, UT.

Roper, Margaret W., "Echoes of the Sage and Cedars, A Centennial History of Oak City, UT," 1969,self-published, Oak City, UT.

Sessions, Patty Bartlett, *Diaries, 1846-1888,* edited by Donna Toland Stewart, 1997, UT State University Press, Logan, UT.

Van Wagoner, Richard S., "Sidney Rigdon and Me," Journal of Mormon History, Fall, 1996, Mormon History Assn., Layton, UT.

Widstoe, John A., *Evidences and Reconciliations,* 1943, Bookcraft, Salt Lake City, UT.

Wells, Emmeline, "Woman's Exponent Vol. 37," October, 1908, LDS Women of the Past, Personal Impressions.

World Book Encyclopedias, 1968, Field Enterprises, Chicago, IL.

Women's Voices, various authors, 1982, Deseret Book, Salt Lake City, UT.

Young, Roger K., *As a Thief in the Night,* 1996, self-published.

Periodicals

Deseret News, as cited, Salt Lake City, UT.

"Hosanna," February, Vol II, April 1997,Vol. III, St. Louis, MO (LDS publication).

"LDS Church News," September 6, 1997, p. 3; June 7, 1997, p. 5; May 24, 1997, p. 9.

Ensign magazine, June, 1979.

Appendices

The following are found in the "Long Journal of Edward Partridge," LDS Church Archives, except as noted. Compiled by Edward Partridge Jr., Fillmore, Utah, 1878.

Appendix A

Significant events in the life of Edward, Lydia Partridge to 1845

1793	27 Aug	Edward born in Pittsfield, Berkshire, MA.
	27 Sept	Lydia Clisbee born in Marlboro, Middlesex, MA.
1809		Edward apprenticed 4 years to hatter at age 16. Worked with Asa Marvin in New York and later bought him out.
1813		"At age of 20 had become disgusted with the religious world and saw no beauty comeliness or loveliness in the character of the God that was preached up by the sects." Was satisfied that God lived, that the scriptures were or divine origin, and made them the touchstone of life... (Biographical Ency, — LDS pp. 218-222.).
1819	22 Aug	Lydia and Edward married in Knoxville, OH, both age 25.
???		Edward established business in Painesville near Lake Erie. Becomes quite well-to-do. Builds good home, a shop and a barn. Owns two lots adjoining the public square and a twenty-acre wood lot adjoining the town (see Partridge Bulletin #7, Emily Young diary, for detailed description).
1820	20 Apr	Eliza Maria born in Painesville, OH.
1822	2 Jan	Harriet Pamelia born in Painesville.
1824	28 Feb	Emily Dow born in Painesville. Named after Edward's sister Emily.
1827	8 Jan	Caroline Ely born in Painesville.
1828		Lydia and Edward baptized as Campbellites by Sidney Rigdon at Mentor.
1829	16 Nov	*Painesville Telegraph* reports arrival in the area of Oliver Cowdery and others, as missionaries of the restored gospel. In its report the *Telegraph* commented that one of the missionaries "pretends to have seen angel." The use of the plural term indicates that Cowdery claimed ministrations from other angels than Moroni — presumably John the Baptist, Peter, James, and John. Continued the *Telegraph: The name of the person here, who pretends to have a divine mission and to have seen and conversed with angels is Cowdery"* (*Joseph Smith, the Man and the Seer, Hyrum Andrus,* pp. 85-86).

1830	fall	Missionaries (Parley P. Pratt, Oliver Cowdery, Peter Whitmer, Jun and Ziba Peterson) call on Partridge home. Edward calls them impostors, refuses Book of Mormon and sends them away. Later sent man after them to get a book.
		Mother Lydia baptized by Parley P. Pratt in Painesville.
		Sidney Rigdon, Campbellite preacher, baptized in Kirtland, OH.
	11 Dec	Edward baptized in Seneca River, Fayette, NY by Joseph Smith.
	Dec	Edward ordained elder by Sidney Rigdon.
1830	8 May	Lydia born in Painesville.
1831	1 Feb	Edward and Rigdon return to Kirtland, accompanied by Joseph and Emma.
	3 Feb	Church to gather in Kirtland area. Revelation received to call Edward as bishop (D&C 41). Compared by Lord to Nathanael of old.
	9 Feb	J. Smith receives D&C 42 on Law of Consecration. Edward, as first bishop, was to "leave his business and devote his entire time to the affairs of the church in putting the Law of Consecration into operation among the Saints (see "Restored Church," Berrett, p. 115).
		Edward had distinction of being called as a bishop sooner after his baptism than anyone else in this dispensation.
	3 Jun	Ordained high priest by Lyman Wight at conference held at Kirtland.
	19 Jun	Left for Missouri with others under direction of Lord to consecrate land there (D&C 52).
	mid Jul	Arrive Independence, Jackson County.
	Aug	Instructed this was "land of their residence" and should bring family here and settle.
	4 Aug	Dedicated site of future temple at Independence.
	6 Aug	Wrote letter to Lydia: "I have a strong desire to return to Painesville this fall, but must not; you know I stand in an important station, and as I am occasionally chastened I sometimes feel as though I must fall; not to give up the cause, but to fear my station is above what I can perform to the acceptance of my Heavenly Father. I hope that you and I may so conduct ourselves as to at last land our souls in the haven of eternal rest. Pray for me that I may not fail."
1832	26 Apr	On behalf of church, Bishop Partridge gave to President Smith the right hand of fellowship (Doc. History).
		During intermission a difficult of hardness which had existed between Edward and Elder Rigdon was amicably settled.
1833		Family moves to Jackson County.
	25 Jun	Edward Jr. born Independence, MO.
	20 Jul	"George Simpson and two other mobbers" entered house, dragged him out. Russel Hicks, named apparent head man of mob. Said his word was law of county and Edward must agree to leave or suffer consequences. "I answered that if I must suffer for my religion it was no more than others had done before me; that I was not conscious of having injured any one in the county, therefore I would not consent to leave it." Successfully pleaded not to be stripped naked in the street. Man named Davies and another tarred and feathered him (Edward's journal quoted in Biograph. Ency. p.220).
		"I...was willing to suffer for the sake of Christ, but to leave the county,

I was not then willing" (HC 1:390-91).

Edward wrote: "I bore my abuse with so much resignation and meekness that it appeared to astound the multitude, who permitted me to retire in silence, many looking solemn, their sympathies having been touched...and as to myself, I was so filled with the spirit and love of God, that I had no hatred toward my persecutors or anyone else (ibid).

	Oct	Mob contract signed by Edward and others agrees to leave Jackson Cty. Jan 1843.
	5 Nov	Driven from home, house burned by mob.
	13 Nov	Both Lydia and Edward mention stars falling "like snowflakes," Flee to Clay County.
	Nov	Edward attempts to obtain redress for grievances of church
1834		Edward serves mission to Eastern States.
1835		Caroline Ely baptized by Peter Whitmer.
	Oct	Edward stops in Kirtland.
	7 Nov	Joseph Smith receives message from Lord re: "well pleased with my servants Isaac Morley and Edward Partridge...their sins are forgiven them...attend school of prophets and solemn assembly for wise purpose in me" (D&C).
1836	27 Mar	Dedicated Kirtland temple.
	4 May	Started back for Clay County.
	fall	People of Clay County offer to buy lands of Mormons if they will leave. Moved to Caldwell County.

Eliza teaches school 30 miles away. During three months there she heard nothing from family.

Far West was laid out and became the temporary gathering place of saints. Growing numbers in this area, plus expansion into Daviess and Carroll counties, revived jealousies and mob spirit.

Eliza learns tailoring trade, which proves to help greatly later on.

	6 Dec	Church votes to give Edward $1.50 day for service as bishop
		Edward files suit against Jackson County for lawyer expenses.
1838	4 Jul	Edward lays southeast cornerstone of Far West Temple.
	6 Aug	Daviess County election riot.
	25 Sept	Conflict with Gov. Boggs, letters, etc. begins.
	Oct	Battle of Crooked River.
	fall	Far West sieged, sacked. Forced to sign "deed of trust" (see Edward's description Bio. Ency., p. 221).
	fall	Held in Richmond prison three weeks (description, p. 221).

Gov. Boggs issues extermination order. Gen. Clark appears willing to carry it out.

	winter	Family moves to Quincy, IL with help of King Follet. Edward joins them when released from prison.
1839	summer	Move to Nauvoo.
	5 Oct	Edward named bishop of Upper Ward; Newel K. Whitney and Vinson Knight assigned to Middle and Lower Wards.

Family lives in William Law's home. Edward builds stable and moves family there to be closer to his work while building home.

1840	16 May	Harriet Pamelia (age 19) dies suddenly in Nauvoo. Edward had sent a man to notify Eliza, who drives all night and reaches Nauvoo just before Harriet dies.
		Edward bedridden with pleurisy.
	27 May	Edward dies (J. Smith writes "He lost his life in consequence of the Missouri persecutions, and he is one of that number whose blood will be required at their hands."
	30 May	William Law takes Edwards family into his home to stay until the house Edward started was finished — about three weeks. He also doctered Lydia who was very sick.
		Eliza goes to work in tailor shop and paid three dollars a week.
1841		Lydia Clisbee Partridge marries William Huntington, as she finds it very hard to get along alone. He is referred to by family as "Father Huntington." Eliza writes: "He was a very good man and very good and kind to my mother and her children."
1842	5 Apr	Elizabeth Buxton born in Sheffield, ENG.
1843	4 Mar	Emily Dow married to Joseph Smith by Heber C. Kimball; live in home with him and Emma. Emily writes, "There was no more bitter enemy than Emma from that time."
	8 Mar	Eliza marries Joseph Smith.
1844	27 Jun	Prophet martyred. Eliza living with Coolidge family at time, and remains with them until she marries Amasa Lyman.
	6 Sept	Caroline Ely becomes Amasa Lyman's second wife.
1845	Sept	Eliza marries Amasa Lyman.
	17 Oct	Amasa Lyman marries by proxy Harriet Pamelia.
	14 Jul	First born of Eliza and Amasa, Don Carlos, was born in wagon at Florence, NB.
	12 Dec	Don Carlos died in Florence, NB. Buried east side of Platte River.

Appendix B

Author's note: the following are copied as written except for minor punctuation changes to help today's reader. It should be remembered that it was not the style of the times to end every sentence with a period.

Jackson County, August 5, 1831

Letter to His Wife

Dear Wife,

You will perceive by the commandments received here (which our brethren will carry home) that brothers Morley, Correll [sic] and Phelps and myself are to plant ourselves and our families here as soon as consistent. You will likewise perceive that we are left to our own agreement how we will manage about getting our families here. Brother Gilbert and Phelps think they must return to procure the necessaries for their establishments. And as Brother Gilbert or I must be here to attend the sales in December and not knowing that he can get back by that time I have thought it advisable to stay here for the present, contrary to my expectations. It is expected by Brothers Correll and Phelps that they shall return this fall to their land with Gilbert's family and if you can get ready and come with them (together with Brother Morleys family and Brother Corrells, although Brother Correll has not yet arrived) it will probably be for the best. If you should come with them, I may never go again to that land, except the settlement of my affairs should demand it, and should you come or not, and my affairs need me there, and Brother Gilbert arrives in them, I can return this winter, and back here in the spring.

We cannot get very well prepared for houses this fall, and if I knew that I should go back this winter, for your comfort and convenience, I would rather you should stay and come with me in the spring. But this I shall leave to your own discretion and the advice of friends. I will now give you can idea of things to fetch and things to leave or sell. Here follows in particular domestic matters Samuel H. Smith and Brother Calhoon arrived last night, baptized none on the way. When I left Painesville, I told people I was coming back and bade none a farewell but for a short time, consequently I feel a great desire to return once more, and bid

Your connexion [sic] and my friends and acquaintances an eternal farewell, unless they should be willing to forsake all for the sake of Christ, and be gathered with the saints of the most high God.

Aug. 6

We have to suffer and shall for some time, many privations here which you and I have not been much used to for years. I hardly know what to advise you about coming this fall, I should like to have you come with Brother Phelps', Morleys' and Corrells' families even this far, but were a number of families coming in the spring so that you could come as cheap. You would be far better accommodated there than here, but I should advise our brethren to stay there until commanded to move...

Our brethren here have begun a house, but we proceed slowly for we have had to work to great disadvantages, those who come from the east are all crowded into two small log houses. Old Mrs. Knight is very low, probably will not live long. Last Thursday we had conference, and a number are to start back immediatel. When the rest arrive we are to hold another conference. Brothers Morley and Correlle [sic] will not return, and if Brother Seth Griffin feels to stay here I suppose he will, for they want his work. Our Brethren, here are in, general good health and spirits. I have a strong desire to return to Painesvilles this fall but must not. You know I stand in an important station, and as I am occasionally chastened I sometimes fear my station is above what I can perform to the acceptance of my Heavenly Father. I hope you and I may conduct ourselves as at last to land souls in the heaven of eternal rest. Pray that I may not fall, I might write more but must not, farewell for the present.

Edward Partridge

Appendix C

Kirtland Geauga Co., Ohio, Nov. 2nd 1835

Excerpts from Edward's Letter to his Wife

My Dear Wife,

I have once more arrived safe at this place, and I find it a general time of health. I have received your letter dated July 29th by mail, and also one dated Sept. 5th and 6th together with, a line from Eliza, you inform me that you and the children were sick. I was somewhat disappointed at this intelligence as I had fondly anticipated that you would be blessed with health in my absence, from what is in by blessings but all blessings are conditional, and perhaps if none of you had been unfaithful I may have been, and notwithstanding you have been sick it also is a chastisement upon me. I have had great anxiety for two or three days past to be with you, to comfort and take care of you, and things round about. Dr. Calvin Beebe arrived here last evening safe and well and desires to be remembered back to his family. He informed me that you and the children were better. This intelligence comforted my heart. I fondly hope and pray that you are all restored to health at this. Brother L. Wight arrived today well, Bro. C. Beebe left him at Cincinnati. Bro. H. Redfield and Chapman Duncan have not arrived yet. Bro. Morley will not arrive this 10 or 15 days. It was quite muddy and he left me at Jordon, and I came in from there by water, with the few goods we had received. He was well and in good spirits...

I have enjoyed good health the past summer. I should really like to be with you this winter, but President Smith says it is my duty to attend the school this winter. I expect that the House will not be finished till towards spring, though they push it as fast as they can. The lower windows are mostly in, and the lower room principally lathed. They are preparing to commence plastering soon. Bro. C. Beebe's wife's mother has been baptized. Bishop Whineys [sic] father and mother joined last week. You want me to give you advice and directions what to do, and in answer I say respecting the yearlings, if you want one or both of them for meat kill them, and if you don't want to kill them, sell them and also the calves if you think best. If you have not keeping for them, of necessity you must sell them. You can advise with Bro. Burk as to price etc. and get him to assist you. As to the amount of corn you will want it depends in part how much you want for the stock. If corn is cheap it will be well to buy a number of barrels. I should like to have one of the young creatures, either yearling or calf, kept for a beef next fall, but if you sell them, I can probably buy one. Wheat—you want about one bushel a week. You need not lay in a very large stock as probably it will not rise much. I expect to be home early in the spring, and can buy after I come. Pork and lard and honey, you must buy what you think you shall want. I shall send in this letter ten dollars, and if you are likely to need more before spring you will inform me, and I will endeavor to send it to you. If you need winter clothing, and have means to buy with you must buy. I know of no opportunity to send you any, neither have I any on hand, that are suitable for you if I had an opportunity to send. Bro. Calvin tells me that you did not know how I expected you to proceed to pay the taxes. I either told you or wrote you that i wanted you to call on Bro. Burk to get him to see to it, and if I am not much mistaken I spoke to him about it before I came from there. I wrote in one of my letters, to have you get Bro. Slade to help you to such things as you wanted, you can call on him and if the horses has earned anything the past season, he will probably help you. Nov. 5th Bro. Morley has arrived this day and is well, l have seen to Mr. Leis, they are well. Mr. Lee is as rude as ever. I did not have much opportunity with Thebe married about six weeks ago to one Cass who dies a week after. So she is left a young widow. She appears somewhat cast down. Phebe said she believed Axa's health was some better than it was last spring.

9th

I have just returned from Cleaveland, our friends there are well. Sister Hebard is strong in the faith, and he (Mr. Hebard) is not hard. Lewis is willing this week should be true and he is considerably believing. Sister H. Intends to come to this place and be baptized the first opportunity. I want Bro. Burk to keep watch and see if our lawyers in managing our suits, should fail of throwing the costs upon our enemies, and thereby throw a bill of costs upon us, and inform us immediately that we may contrive to pay it, and save our land in Jackson County, from falling into the hands of the mob.

10th

The noted imposter Matthias arrived at this place yesterday, He proves to be an infidel. He wears a long beard etc. etc. The weather is fine for the season. They have got about 1/3 of the outside of the house plastered. Ten days or two weeks good weather more they will finish it on the outside. They have also began to plaster the lower room inside. If Bro. Ira wants any clothes, he can have any of those that Bro. James H. P. left at our house if they suit him. I shall endeavor to write you from time to time.

I remain your affectionate husband
Edward Partridge

Appendix D

November 2, 1835

Edward Partridge's Letter to His Daughter, Harriet

Harriet My Daughter,

It rejoices me to have you write to me that you are determined to keep the commandments of God. If you live and are faithful you will be permitted to return to Zion with songs of joy. You must not forget to remember your father in your prayers. You say you should be glad to see me. I also should be glad to see all of you, and I trust that I shall see you in this spring if our lives are spared. We must be willing to forsake all things for Christ and the Gospel. I hope you will be patient until it is the will of the Lord that I should return. I as glad to hear that the children have been to school, but was sorry to hear that any were sick.

I remain your loving father,
Edward Partridge

Appendix E

Kirtland, Ohio May 2, 1833

Joseph Smith's Letter to Edward Partridge

Beloved Brother Edward,

I commence answering your letter and sincere request to me, by begging your pardon for not having addressed you, more particularly in letters which I have written to Zion, for I have always felt, as though a letter written to anyone in authority in Zion, would be the property of all, and it mattered but little to whom it was directed. But I am satisfied that this is an error, for instruction is given pointedly, and expressly to us, designating our names as individuals seems to have double power and influence over our minds. I am thankful to the Lord for the testimony of his spirit, which he has given me concerning your honesty and sincerity before him, and the Lord loveth you, and also Zion, for he chasteneth whom he loveth, and scourgeth every son and daughter whom he receiveth, and he will not suffer you to be confounded, and of this thing you may rest assured, notwithstanding, all the threatenings of the enemy, and your perils among false brethren, for verily I say unto you, that this is my prayer and I verily believe the prayer of all the saints in Kirtland, recorded in heaven. In these words, Heavenly Father in the name of Jesus thy son, preserve brother Edward, the bishop of thy church, and give him wisdom, knowledge and power, and the holy ghost, that he may impart to thy saints in Zion, their inheritances, and to every man his portion of meat in due season, and now, this is our confidence and record on high, therefore fear not little flock, for it has been your father's good will to give you the kingdom.

Now I will proceed to tell you my views concerning consecration, property, and giving inheritances etc. The law of the Lord, binds you to receive whatsoever property is consecrated, by deed. The consecrated property is considered the residue kept for the Lord's storehouse, and it is given for this consideration, for to purchase inheritances for the poor. This, any man has a right to do agreeable to all laws of our country, to donate, give or consecrate all that he feels disposed to give, and it is your duty, to see that whatsoever is given legally, therefore, it must be given for the consideration of the poor saints, and in this way no man can take any advantage of you in law. Again, concerning inheritances, you are bound by the law of the Lord, to give a deed, securing to him who receives inheritances, his inheritances for an everlasting inheritance, or in other words, to be his individual property, his private stewardship, and (if he sins or transgresses) and should be cut off, out of the church, his inheritance is his still, and he is delivered over to the buffetings of Satan, till the day of redemption.

But the property which he consecrated to the poor for their benefit, and inheritance and stewardship, he cannot obtain again by the law of the Lord. Thus you see the propriety of this law, that rich men cannot have power to disinherit the poor by obtaining again that which they have consecrated which is the residue, signified in the law, that you will find in the second paragraph of the extract from the law, in the second number, and now brother Edward, be assured that we all feel thankful that the brethren in Zion are beginning to humble themselves, and trying to keep the commandments of the Lord, which is our prayer to God, you may all be able to do and no, may the grace of God be with all. Amen.

Joseph Smith Jun.

Appendix F

November 1833

Edward Partridge Letter to Joseph Smith After Expulsion from Jackson County

Beloved Brother Joseph,

I set myself down this evening to write you a few lines, I shall not attempt to give you a full history of what has happened unto us within a few days past for I suppose that Bro. Phelps has given you the particulars. It sufficeth to say that Bro. Corrill and myself are living within three miles of Liberty, and about 10 miles from Independence. Most of our Brethren have left Jackson Co. many have come to this Co. some have gone south and some east. When it was concluded that we would go, there appeared to be a spirit almost universal for leaving the land forthwith our move has been speedy and we have had many inconveniences to encounter. The Lord for the most part, as yet, has given us very favorable weather, many are living in tents and shanties not being able to procure houses as yet. We are in hopes we shall be able to return to our houses and lands before a great while, but how this is to be accomplished is all in the dark to us as yet. Bro. Parley has prophesied that we shall be enabled to return to our houses by the First of next January and enjoy the fruits of our labor and none to molest or make afraid, he says he was constrained to prophesy and if ever he spoke by the Spirit of God he then did and if it does not come to pass we call him a false prophet. The next night after this prophecy was delivered from one or two o'clock till day light on the morning of the 13th at Nov appeared an extraordinary phenomenon. The heavens were literally filled with meteors or shooting stars as they are called. I was encamped on the north side of the Missouri opposite Independence and it appeared to us that they shot off every way from us, none coming directly down, though it is said that they struck the ground in Independence and other places round about. I viewed them for more than an hour before daylight and probably saw thousands. At one time in the N. E. there appeared probably 40 or 100 at one time, they streamed down almost as thick as rain which appears at a distance when the sun shines upon it. During this sight our people rejoiced, but the worlds people were much frightened. There has some other signs appeared of late, and rumor says many, but I put no confidence in the reports of our enemies. If we are delivered and permitted to return to our homes it must be by the interposition of God, for we can see no prospect of help from government, and it appears to me that naught but the judgment of God will open the way for our return. Some of our brethren have their fears, that we shall be driven from city to city and from synagog to synagog and few be left to receive an inheritance in the land and this probably will be the case, unless we are soon restored back. For notwithstanding that many are kind to us in this Co. yet we have every reason to believe that they will shortly be stirred up against us, and want to drive us further. The world people are very desirous to have us sell the lands, and since you advise us not to, I do not want to, but if we are to be driven about for years I can see no use in keeping our possessions here. Some of our brethren who have given me money to buy lands with, are desirous to receive a deed of some land, and I have thought it best to give deeds to such as are anxious to have them. I want your advice upon this subject of the land, and also I want wisdom and light on many subjects in this time of trial. We have made two attempts to get a peace warrant. The first before a justice one of the mob. He at first refused, but after consulting with some others of the mob, he consented. We however sent to Lexington 40 miles east to the circuit Judge, and after quite a struggle made out to obtain. But when the brethren came back with it, we had agreed to go away, and the mob, or militia as they were called, were raging with great fury, and we have done nothing with it, neither do we believe it would be of any use, to try to enforce it now. Our lawyers say it can do us no good in their opinion. As to our suits for damage we were expecting to start a number between this and the next term, which is in February next. There has been no writ taken out as yet. Since our removal we have not been able to get together so as to have a council of High Priests and advise with one another what is best to do. It would seem that the prospect is bad respecting our having justice done us by any course we may pursew [sic] Justice would give us the County of Jackson, almost we believe but this would take years to accomplish unless our damages could be settled by arbitration, that is, leaving the case to judicious disinterested men. There is another way we might obtain the land, by natural means that is this. Could we obtain money by loan or from brethren that were able we might butt out the most of the inhabitants in all probability and let them leave the county. But this would take many thousand dollars. After looking at the whole. I am of the opinion that unless God works for his people, and displays his power, in some way or another, we cannot return to the land again. My mind is to have the disciples all leave the land, and see if God will not pour out his judgements in some way upon that wicked people. Rumors are afloat that it is with difficulty that the Indians are restrained from coming upon the people. As to this I know nothing about it and I place no great confidence in rumors. I hope err this there may have been a comforting word from the Lord through you, but be this as it may, I am anxious to hear from you. I heart [sic] your brother in Christ."

Edward Partridge

Appendix G

Kirtland, Ohio, May 4, 1835

Patriarchal Blessing received by Edward Partridge

Edward Partridge was born at Pittsfield, Berkshire Co., Massachusetts August 27th 1793 and received the following patriarchal blessing, under the hand of J. S. the evangelist.

Bro. Partridge let thy heart sink down in humility; give thyself up into the hands of thy God and be willing to receive the blessings that he is willing to bestow upon thee. I lay my hands upon thy head in the name of Jesus Christ and confirm a patriarchal blessing upon thee because thou hast no father that can bestow it upon thee. I confirm upon thee the same blessings which are confirmed upon Abraham and Isaac and Jacob; and Joseph and his posterity; and they shall rest upon thee and thy children after thee unto the latest generations, for thou art a chosen man of God, who did look upon thee before the foundation of the world, and has set thee apart to do good in his cause. Thou art of the seed of Abraham through the loins of Joseph and the tribe of Ephraim. The Lord will bless thee with the ministration of angels because of the integrity of thy heart and thy willingness to obey his commandments. Thou art one of the horns of Joseph that are to push the people together from the ends of the earth. And thou shalt be instrumental in a saving, and some of thy friends shall be given thee if thou art faithful. Thy name shall be sealed among the sanctified; The Lord will preserve thy life till a good old age, and thou shalt also live to see the heavens opened, for thou hast desired this thing, and shalt see the Son of man in the flesh. Thy heart shall be enlarged from this very hour; thou shalt have great wisdom to execute thy mission and calling. Thou shalt perform great miracles and shall have faith even like unto the brother of Jared.

Thy wife shall be blessed also and received the desire of her heart; she shall have night visions and thereby know of thy welfare in thine absence; thy family shall be preserved in health and thou shalt return to enjoy their society after thou hast performed thy mission. Thy tongue shall soon be loosened and thou shalt have great power to speak beyond any thing of which thou hast thought. Thy name is written in heaven and will not be blotted out except for willful transgression. Thou shalt live to see the redemption of Zion and rejoice upon the goodly lord, thou shall inherit it and thy seed after thee to the latest generations while the earth remains. Thou shalt stand in thy office until thou art weary of it and shall desire to resign it that thou mayest rest for a little season. I seal upon thee those blessings in the name of Jesus Christ of Nazareth, Amen...

Appendix H

Edward's Prayer at Far West

O Lord look down in mercy upon thy people, who are afflicted and oppressed. How long O Lord, wilt thou suffer the enemy to oppress thy saints. Destruction hath come upon us like a wild wing in the which thou hast verified thy word. for thou didst forewarn us that it would come, and behold thy word is fulfilled. The enemy came upon us, to drive us from the state of Missouri, or exterminate us, but thou O Lord didst stay their hands from killing us though numbers were massacred, and thou didst send forth uncommon severe frost and snow, and by that means save us, as a people, from being driven out at the time appointed. But thou didst suffer the enemy unlawfully to take thy servant, together with scores of others, who drove us like dumb asses from our homes in a cold dreary and meloncholly time. We were confined in a large open room where the cold northern blast penetrated freely; our fires were small, and our allowance for wood and for food scanty; they gave us not even a blanket to lie upon, our beds were the cold floor; then thou didst suffer the wicked to tyrannize over us, yea, the vilest of the vile did guard us and treat us like dogs; yet we bore our oppressions without murmuring, but our souls were vexed, both night and day, with their filthy conversation, for they constantly blasphemed thy holy name. Wilt thou not soon cut them off and consign them their portion among hypocrites, and unbelievers? In the midst of our oppression we did call upon thy name, O Lord, and thou didst hear us, and deliver us in some degree, from the hand of oppression, yet the enemy cloth still threaten us, and would fain destroy us, from the face of the earth, but we are in thy hands, O Lord, and we know that the enemy can go no further in oppressing us than thou dost permit. O Lord deliver thou us, from our oppressors, send thy judgments and destroy these who are not willing to let thy servants have a resting place, upon this thy footstool. Save thy people O Lord, save thy people from oppression, and bondage, yea redeem thy Zion, in thine own time redeem it. How long O Lord, shall the enemy be permitted to wear out thy saints, Hasten O Hasten the day, when the ancient of Days shall sit, and power be given thy saints to take and possess the Kingdom even forever and ever Amen.

Appendix I

Edward Partridge Indictments against Missouri

The following is a copy of the statement and account of Edward Partridge against the State of Missouri:

In the year of our Lord 1831 I removed from the State of Ohio to Jackson Co. Missouri. I purchased land and built me a house near the village of Independence where I lived a peaceable inhabitant molesting nobody. On the 20th day of July AD 1833

George Simpson and two other mobbers entered my house (whilst I was sitting with my wife who was then quite feeble my youngest child being then about three weeks old) and compelled me to go with them, soon after leaving my house I was surrounded by about fifty mobbers who escorted me about half a mile to the Public Square where I was surrounded by some two or three hundred more. Russell Hicks Esq. appeared to be the head of the mob. He told me that his word was the law in the county and that I must agree to leave the county or suffer the consequences. I answered that if I must suffer for my religion it was no more than others had done before me; that I was not conscious of having injured any one in the county therefore I could not consent to leave it. Mr. Hicks then proceeded to strip off my clothes and was disposed to strip them all off. I strongly protested against being stripped naked in the street, when some more humane than the rest inteferred and I was permitted to ware (sic) my shirt and pantaloons. Tar and feathers were then brought and a man by the name of — Davies with the help of another daubed me with tar from the crown of my head to my feet after which feathers were thrown over me. For this abuse I have never received any satisfaction, although I commenced a suit against some of them for 40000$ damage and paid my lawyers six hundred dollars to carry it on. I also paid near two hundred dollars to get a change of venue. My lawyers after getting their pay of me made a compromise with the defendants without my consent and threw my case out of court, without given me any damages, by their agreeing to pay the costs, which they have never paid that I know of, and I never could prevail upon my lawyers to collect them for me, though they agreed so to do.

Nov. 1833 I was compelled by a mob to leave Jackson County at which time I held the title to two thousand one hundred and thirty six acres of land all lying in that county and also two village lots situated in the village of Independence. Such have been the threats of the people of that county that I have never to this day dared to go on to ...my lands there, although I still own some there yet.

From Jackson I moved to Clay county where I lived till the fall of 1836 when I moved my family to what is now Caldwell County. There I purchased land and built houses, where I lived till last winter, when in conformity with the order of Gov. Boggs and the threats of Gen. Clark I moved my family to the state of Illinois, at which time I held the title to forty acres of land in Clay County, and more than four fifths of the lots in the Town of Far West Caldwell County which was laid out one mile square and was settling very rapidly. I had five houses and one barn in the Town. I also held eight hundred and sixty eight acres of land in Caldwell county. The property in Caldwell county had sunk to a mere trifle in consequence of our Church not being protected there, I give the following for a sample. I bought a house last summer in Far West and have twelve hundred dollars for it. After I bought it a well was dug and other repairs made amounting to between fifty and a hundred dollars; this property has lately been sold by my agent and only brought one hundred dollars. Another house and lot, which last summer I would not have been willing to have, taken three hundred dollars for, has been sold by my agent and brought only thirty dollars, however I cannot that property there will remain so low for long. Whilst our society lived in Jackson and Clay counties there never was one of them to the best of my knowledge ever convicted of any criminal offenses and a lawsuit of any kind was very rare. Although they were accused of many unlawful things, especially in Jackson Court when at the same time the administration of the laws was in their own hands, but for the want of anything legal against us they proceeded against us illegally, and not only drove us from our lands and homes in Jackson County, but kept us from them, and this order of things was suffered by the authorities and people of the state, to remain year after year, until at last for the want of protection against that spirit of mobocracy, we have been compelled to leave the state. I lived near three years in Clay Co. within a few miles of the line of Jackson Co. and no man from Jackson County or anywhere else brought any law suit of any kind whatever against me during the time, I feel that the state of Missouri ought to pay an immense sum for damages for not protecting us in the first place in our rights in Jackson Co. and in the second place in not granting us protection in the state.

Last fall I was taken from my home in Far west Missouri by Gen. Clark without any civil process and driven off to Richmond Ray County thirty miles and kept a prisoner between three and four weeks before I was liberated for which I think the state of Missouri ought to pay me a round sum.

The following charges I make against the state of Missouri for losses sustained leaving my damages to be competed by others. My losses in Jackson County Missouri in stripping my land of timber, destruction of my house, corn, potatoes, etc. etc. of $150,000.00) My loss in paying lawyers to carry my suits $950.00.

My loss or expected loss on my land houses and village lots in Caldwell in consequence of having to leave that 5000.00. My loss for time and expense of moving a large family cut of the state sacrifice of furniture etc. 400.00. My loss for having taken by the Militia a number of guns pistols and sword $100.00 My loss in the destruction of corn, hay, sheep and one fat horned bears. 42.00 Total 3699300 Quincy, Illinois May 15, 1839.

I certify that that above statements are correct according to the best of my knowledge and belief.

Edward Partridge

Sworn and Subscribed before me this 15th day of May AD 1839 CM Woods Clerk Circuit Court Adams County State of Illinois

Appendix J

March 4, 1840

Petition for Redress to the US Senate

25th Congress, 1st Session. Senate. In the Senate of the United States. March 4, 1840. Submitted, laid on the table, and ordered to be printed. Mr. Wall made the following report:

The Committee on the Judiciary, to whom was referred the memorial of a delegation of the Latter-day Saints, commonly called Mormons, report:

The petition of the memorialists sets forth, in substance, that a portion of their sect commence a settlement in the county of

Jackson, in the State of Missouri, in the summer of 1831 ; that they bought lands, built houses, erected churches, and established their homes, and engaged in all the various occupations of life: that they were expelled from that county in 1833, by a mob, under circumstances of great outrage, cruelty, and oppression, and against all law, and without any offense of their part, and to the destruction of property to the amount of $120,000: that the society thus expelled amounted to about 1,200 souls: that no compensation was ever made for the destruction of their property in Jackson: that after their expulsion from Jackson county, they settled in Clay county, on the opposite side of the Missouri river, where they purchased lands, and entered others at the land office, where they resided peaceably for three years, engaged in cultivations and other useful and active employments, when the mob again threatened their peace, lives, and property; and they became alarmed, and finally made a treaty with the citizens of Clay county that they should purchase their lands, and the Mormons should remove; which was complied with on their part, and the Mormons removed to the county of Caldwell, where they took up their abode, and re-established their settlement, not without heavy pecuniary losses and other inconveniences: that the citizens of Clay county never paid them for their lands, except for a small part. They remained in Caldwell from 1836 until the fall of 1838, and during that time had acquired, by purchase from the Government, the settlers, and pre-emptioners, almost all the lands in the county of Caldwell, and a portion of the lands in Daviess and Carroll counties, the former county being almost entirely settled by the Mormons, and they were rapidly filling up the two latter counties. Those counties, when the Mormons first commenced their settlement, were, for the most part, wild and uncultivated, and they had converted them into large and well-improved farms, well stocked. Lands had risen in value to $100 and even $25 per acre, and those counties were rapidly advancing in cultivation and wealth: that in August, 1838, a riot commenced, growing out of an attempt of a Mormon to vote, which resulted in creating great excitement and the perpetration of many scenes of lawless outrage, which are set forth in the petition that they were finally compelled to fly from those counties, and on the 11th October, 1838, they sought safety by that means, with their families, leaving many of their effects behind: that they had previously applied to the constituted authorities of Missouri for protection, but in vain. They allege that they were pursued by the mob; that conflicts ensued; deaths occurred on each side; and finally, a force was organized, under the authority of the Governor of the State of Missouri, with orders to drive the Mormons from the State, or exterminate them. The Mormons thereupon determined to make no further resistance but to submit themselves to the authorities of the State. Several of the Mormons were arrested and imprisoned on a charge of treason against the State; and the rest, amounting to about 15,000 souls, fled into other states, principally in Illinois, where they now reside.

The petition is drawn up at great length, and sets forth, with feeling and eloquence, the wrongs of which they complain; justifies their own conducts, and aggravate that of those whom they call their persecutors, and concludes by saying that they see no redress, unless it be obtained of the Congress of the United States, to whom they make their solemn last appeal as American citizens, as Christians, and as men. To which decision they say they will submit.

The committee have examined the case presented by the petition, and heard the views urged by their agent, with care and attention; and, after full examination and consideration, unanimously concur in the opinion that the case presented for their investigation is not such a one as will justify or authorize any interposition by this Government. The wrongs complained of are not alleged to be committed by any of the officers of the United States, or under the authority of its Government in any manner whatever. The allegations in the petition relate to the acts of the citizens, and inhabitants, and authorities of the State of Missouri, of which State the petitioners were at the time citizens or inhabitants. The grievances complained of in the petition are alleged to have been done within the territory of the State of Missouri. The committee under these circumstances, have not considered themselves justified in inquiring into the truth or falsehood of the facts charged in the petition. If they are true, the petitioners must seek relief in the courts of judicature of the State of Missouri, or of the United States, which has the appropriate jurisdiction to administer full and adequate redress for the wrongs complained of, and doubtless will do so fairly and impartially; or, the petitioners may, if they see proper, apply to the justice and magnanimity of the State of Missouri — an appeal which the committee feel justified in believing will never be made in vain by the injured or oppressed. It can never be presumed that a State either wants the powers, or lacks the disposition, to redress the wrongs of its own citizens committed within her own territory, whether they proceed from the lawless acts of her officers, or any other persons.

The committee therefore report that they recommend the passage of the following resolution:

Resolved: That the Committee on the Judiciary be discharged from the further consideration of the memorial in this case; and that the memorialists have leave to withdraw the papers which accompany their memorial.

Appendix K

Recording of Jackson County temple lot sale by Lydia Partridge, May 5, 1848

See next page.

Source: State record vault, Jefferson City, Mo.

To all people to whom these presents shall come greeting Know ye that we Lydia Partridge widow of Edward Partridge deceased Eliza M Partridge Emily D Partridge and Caroline E Partridge heirs of the said Edward Partridge deceased now living in Pottawatomie County &c for and in consideration of the sum of three hundred dollars received to our full satisfaction of James Pool of the County of Jackson in the State of Missouri do give grant bargain sell confirm and quit claim unto the said party of the second part the following described peice or parcel of Land being a part of the South East quarter of section three in Township Number Forty nine of Range No thirty two in the aforesaid Jackson County Missouri bounded and described as follows to wit commencing on the South Line of said quarter section forty poles 10 from the South East corner of said quarter section at the corner of a certain peice of Land sold by said Flournoy & wife to one Lewis Jones and from thence running west one hundred and twenty Poles to south west corner of said quarter section; thence North sixteen poles and ten links thence North Forty degrees East ten poles thence North twenty one degrees East fourteen poles thence North Fifteen degrees East twenty poles thence North forty two degrees East thirty four poles thence North Fifty five degrees East thirty four poles thence North Sixty four degrees East forty poles thence North seventy degrees East seventeen Poles and fifteen Links to the corner of a certain tract of Land sold by said Flournoy & wife to one B M Hensley and from thence due South one hundred and seventy two poles and seventeen links to the place of beginning containing Sixty three acres and forty three one hundred and sixtieths of an acre be the same more or less To have & to hold the above granted bargained and quit-claimed premises with all and singular the rights privaliges and appurtenances thereunto in any wise belonging or appurtaining unto him the said James Pool his heirs and assigns forever to his and their own propper use and behoof and we the said party of the first part for ourselves our heirs and assigns covenant with the said James Pool his heirs and assigns that at and until the enseeling of these presents we are well seized of the premises as a good indefeasible Estate in fee simple and have good right to bargain and sell and quit-claim the same in manner & form as is above written and that be the same.

In presence of   Lydia Partridge (seal)
Allen Atwood   Eliza M Partridge (seal)
Mathew C. West   Emily D Partridge (seal)
State of Missouri   Caroline E Partridge (seal)
County of Atchison } Be it Remembered that on this fifth day of May in the year Eighteen hundred and forty eight before me A W Bradford clerk of the circuit court within and for the County of Atchison aforesaid personally came Lydia Partridge Eliza M Partridge Emily D Partridge and Caroline E Partridge who are personally known to me to be the same persons whose names are subscribed to the foregoing instrument of writing as parties thereto and acknowledged the same to be their voluntary act & deed for the purposes therein mentioned In Testimony whereof I have hereunto set my hand and affixed my private seal. (there being no seal of court provided) At office the day and year last aforesaid

                    A W Bradford Clk &c

The foregoing deed from Lydia Partridge & others to James Pool together with the acknowledgment thereon endorsed was deposited and duly Recorded in my office on the 16th day of June A D 1848
                Samuel D Lucas Recorder

Appendix L

Unrecorded revelation to Edward Partridge

Revelation Concerning Edward Partridge and His Family

Kirtland, Ohio, January 7, 1838. [five days before the Prophet's flight from Kirtland the following revelation was recorded:]

"Thus saith the Lord. My servant Edward Partridge and his house shall be numbered with the blessed and Abraham their father; and his name shall be held in sacred remembrance. And again, thus saith the Lord, let my people beware of dissensions among them, lest the enemy have power over them. Awake, my shepherds, and warn my people, for behold the wolf cometh, to destroy them. Receive him not."

This revelation is not contained in the D&C, nor in J. S. History, but was found among the private papers of Bishop Partridge ("Contributor," Vol. VI, p. 8).

Appendix M

Written by Edward Partridge

Let Zion in Her Beauty Rise

Let Zion in her beauty rise;
Her Light begin to shine.
Ere long her King will rend the skies,
Majestic and divine,
The Gospel spreading through the land,
A People to prepare
To meet the Lord and Enoch's band,
Triumphant in the air.

Ye heralds, sound the golden trump
To earth's remotest bound
Go spread the news from pole to pole
In all the nations round:
That Jesus in the clouds above,
With hosts of angels, too,
Will soon appear, his Saints to save,
His enemies subdue.

That glorious rest will then commence
Which prophets did fortell,
When Saints will reign with Christ on earth,
And in His presence dwell
A thousand years, oh, glorious day!
Dear Lord, prepare my heart
To stand with thee on Zion's mount
And never more to part.

Included in first hymnbook. 1835

Appendix N

*Edward/Lydia Partridge Genealogy and family records.
Compiled by author from various sources.*

Edward PARTRIDGE
Born: 26 APR 1683
Place: Hadley, Massachusetts
Marr: 14 MAY 1707
Place:
Died: 26 DEC 1757
Place:

Martha WILLIAMS
Born: 8 OCT 1690
Place: Hatfield, Massachusetts
Died: 26 NOV 1690
Place:

Thomas BIDWELL
Born: 27 DEC 1682
Place: Middletown, Connecticut
Marr: 28 MAR 1707
Place:
Died: 1716
Place: et see

Prudence SCOTT
Born: 1683
Place:
Died: 1 FEB 1763
Place:

Ebenezer DEVOTION
Born: 19 OCT 1684
Place: Roxbury, Massachusetts
Marr: 11 APR 1741
Place:
Died:
Place:

Naomi TAYLOR wife #2
Born: 1695
Place: Westfield Massachusetts
Died: 6 AUG 1730
Place:

Oliver PARTRIDGE
Born: 13 JUN 1712
Place: Hatfield, Massachusetts
Marr: 10 OCT 1734
Place:
Died: 21 JUL 1792
Place:

Anna WILLIAMS
Born: 21 APR 1688
Place: Weston, Massachusetts
Died:
Place:

Adonijah BIDWELL
Born: 18 OCT 1716
Place: Hartford, Connecticut
Marr: 16 OCT 1760 Place:
Died:
Place:

Jemima DEVOTION wife #2
Born: 13 MAY 1727
Place: Suffield, Connecticut
Died: 7 FEB 1771
Place: Montery Massachusetts

William PARTRIDGE
Born: 1753
Place: Hatfield, Massachusetts
Marr: 3 JUN 1787
Place:
Died: 28 OCT 1836
Place:

Edward PARTRIDGE
Born: 27 AUG 1793
Place: Pittsfield, Massachusetts
Marr: AUG 1819
Place:
Died: 27 MAY 1840
Place: Nauvoo, Illinois
Spouse: Lydia CLISBEE

Jemima BIDWELL
Born: 26 JAN 1765
Place: Montery, Massachusetts
Died: 5 APR 1841
Place:

Joseph CLISBEE
Born: 10 NOV 1762
Place: Marlboro, Massachusetts
Marr: 11 JAN 1787
Place:
Died: 1 MAR 1832
Place: Kinsman, Ohio

Ezekial CLISBEE IV
Born: 1740
Place: Boston, Massachusetts
Marr: 13 MAR 1761
Place:
Died: 1820
Place: A. C. New Hampshire

Ezekial CLISBY III
Born: 11 DEC 1715
Place: Boston, S. Massachusetts
Marr:
Died: BEF 18 NOV 1754
Place:

Sarah WHEATON
Born:
Place:
Died:
Place:

Hannah LEWIS
Born: ABT 1742
Place: of Lynn, Massachusetts
Died: ABT 1814
Place: Alstead, New Hampshire

Joseph LEWIS
Born: 1 JAN 1707
Place: Woburn, Massachusetts
Marr:
Died:
Place:

Molly PEARSON
Born:
Place:
Died:
Place:

Lydia Clisbee
Born: 26 SEP 1793
Place: Marlboro, Massachusetts
Marr: AUG 1819
Place:
Died: 9 JUN 1878
Place: Oak City, Millard, Utah
Spouse: Edward PARTRIDGE

Miriam HOWE
Born: 22 SEP 1765
Place: Marlboro, Massachusetts
Died: 10 JUN 1814
Place: Alstead,,Massachusetts

Asa HOWE
Born: 30 NOV 1733
Place: Marlboro, Massachusetts
Marr: 18 MAR 1762
Place:
Died: 1 FEB 1793
Place: Marlboro, Massachusetts

Abraham HOWE
Born: 21 MAR 1698
Place: Marlboro, Massachusetts
Marr: 20 MAY 1724
Place:
Died: 1781
Place:

Rachel RICE
Born: 2 NOV 1703
Place: Marlboro, Massachusetts
Died: 1782
Place:

Rachel GODDARD
Born: 21 APR 1731
Place: Marlboro, Massachusetts
Died: 10 JUN 1814
Place: Marlboro, Massachusetts

William GODDARD
Born: ABT 1706
Place: Watertown, Massachusetts
Marr: 26 JAN 1726
Place:
Died:
Place:

Kezia CLAYES
Born: 8 DEC 1705
Place: Farmingham, Massachusetts
Died:
Place:

Appendix O

Grandchildren of Edward Partridge and Lydia Clisbee

(Courtesy of Edward Partridge Family Assn.)

By Eliza Maria Partridge Lyman
1. Don Carlos Lyman
2. Platte DeAlton Lyman   (Married to Adelia Robison
                                          (Married to Annie Maude Clark
3. Caroline Eliza Lyman   (Married to Volney King
                                          (Married to Thomas Callister
4. Joseph Alvin Lyman   (Married to Nellie Grayson Roper
5. Lucy Zina Lyman   (Married to Lemuel Hardison Redd

By Emily Dow Partridge Young
1. Edward Partridge Young

2. Emily Augusta Young   (Married to Hiram Bradley Clawson
3. Caroline (Carlie) Young   (Married to Mark Croxall
                                            (Married to George Quayle Cannon
4. Joseph Don Carlos Young   (Married to Alice Naomi Dowden
                                            (Married to Marion Penelope Hardy
5. Miriam Young   (Married to Leonard Goodrich Hardy
6. Josephine Young   (Married to Albert Carrington Young
7. Lura Young

By Caroline Ely Partridge Lyman
1. Martha Lydia Lyman   (Married to Alvin Roper

2. Frederic Rich Lyman	(Married to Ann Elizabeth Lovell
3. Annie Lyman	(Married to William Erastus Dutso
	(Married to Anders Peter Anderson
4. Walter Clisbee Lyman	(Married to Sylvia Ann Lovell
	(Married to Elizabeth Finlinson
	(Married to Lucy Halls
	(Married to Leah Larene Brown
5. Harriet Jane Lyman	(Married to John Edmond Lovell

By Lydia Partridge Lyman

1. Edward Leo Lyman	(Married to Mary Miranda Callister
2. Ida Evelyn Lyman	(Married to Hans Joseph Nielson
3. Frank Arthur Lyman	
4. Lydia May Lyman	(Married to Kuman Treharne Jones

Edward Partridge (Jr.) by Sarah Lucretia Clayton

1. Harriet Pamela Partridge	(Married to Albert Heber Kimball
2. Edward C. Partridge	(Married to Janette King
	(Married to Dora May Weaver (Davis)
3. William Clayton Partridge	(Married to Sarah Jane Stott
4. Effie May Partridge	
5. Lewis Amasa Partridge	
6. Ernest DeAlton Partridge	(Married to Elizabeth Mae Truman
7. Stanley Partridge	(Married to Bessie May Wright
8. Raymond Partridge	(Married to Maud Elizabeth Wentz

Edward Partridge (Jr.) by Elizabeth Buxton

1. Emily Partridge	(Married to George Ayears Black
2. John Clisbee Partridge	
3. Charles Partridge	
4. George Arthur Partridge	(Married to Lucy Smith Lyman
5. Don Carlos Partridge	(Married to Louisa Belle Darling
6. Clara Partridge	(Married to David Felshaw Stevens
7. Frank Harvey Partridge	(Married to Savalla Adell Melville
	(Married to Harriett Ann Whicker
8. Mary Aloha Partridge	(Married to Josiah Wilbur Wixom
9. Lydia Maud Partridge	(Married to Clark Kimball

Appendix P

From the Journal of Emily Dow Partridge Young

An Acrostic written by Lydia Clisbee Partridge to her son Edward
(Note: first letters of each line spell "Edward Partridge")

Each day let all thy actions be
Devoid of strife or enmity
Walk in the way thy father trod
Attend his council which was good
Remember in thy youth, thy God
Desire to know his holy word

Prepare thyself thy place to fill
And seek to know thy Master's will
Repent of all thy faults each day
Try to pursue the heavenly way
Refuse not counsel from thy friend
Improve thy time till time shall end
Depart from sin, make truth thy choice
Grim death may come with all his force
Even that day thou mayest rejoice.

(signed) Your Mother.

Index

A

Abraham (Old Testament), 52
Adam and Eve, 75
Adam-Ondi-Ahman, 62, 88
Algernon, Gilbert (and wife of), 10
Allen, Charles, 44
Aninias and Sapphira (New Testament), 107
Arnold, Benedict, 92
Atchison, Gen. David, 48, 91

B

Baptist rules (in Missouri), 56
Beaver pelts, 7
Bennett, John C., 109
Benson, Pres. Ezra Taft, 127
Billings, Titus, 37, 38
Boggs, Lilburn (Gov. Missouri), 31, 47, 79, 91, 93, 95, 96, 97
Boynton, John, 89
Bridger, Jim, 119
Burton, Bishop David F., 104
Buxton, Elizabeth, 131

C

Calvin (Calvinism), 6
Campbellite religion (Disciples of Christ), 1, 2, 9, 34
Carter, Simeon, 45
Church of Christ (Granville Hedreck), 123
Civil War, 65, 76
Clark, Gen. John, 93
Clayton, Sarah Lucretia, 131
Coe, Joseph, 10
Columbus, Christopher, 4

Consecration, Law of (United Order), 28, 29, 31, 32, 35, 38, 53, 54, 71, 90, 107
Corrill, John, 69, 71, 79, 80
Cowdery, Oliver, 2, 9, 15, 16, 45, 89, 90

D

Danites, 92
David (Old Testament), 24
DeClisbe (Clisbee), 8
Doniphan, Gen. Alexander, 48, 82, 91, 93, 101
Dunklin, Gov. Daniel, 49, 59, 82

E

Enoch (Old Testament), 19, 23, 63

F

Faust, President James E., 104, 108
Fillmore (Utah; settled in), 124
Follett, King, 97
Fremont, John C., 119

G

Gilbert, Sidney, 36
Grant, U.S., 131

H

Hare Krishna religion, 39
Harris, Martin, 10
Haun's Mill, 75, 84, 95
Hawaiian (Sandwich) Islands, 130, 132
Hedrekites (see Church of Christ), 123

Higby, E., 80
Hill Cumorah, 78
Hinckley, President Gordon B., 104, 113
Huntington, William (Lydia's husband), 120
Hyde, Orson, 50, 92, 93

I

Independence, Declaration of, 55
Israel, ancient, 5
Israel, children of, 60, 63, 64, 118

J

Jackson, Gen. Andrew, 55
Jews/Jewish Nation, 4, 64, 82, 102
Johnson, Lyman, 89
Johnston's Army, 125
Joshua (Old Testament), 63

K

Kimball, Heber C., 5, 110
Kirtland (Ohio) temple, 78
Knight, Vinson, 102

L

Laman/Lamanite/Indian, 4, 9, 26, 62, 77, 119, 121
Laurence, Sarah and Maria (wives of Joseph Smith), 110, 111
Law, William 109
Lewis & Clark expedition, 119
Lucas, Gen. Samuel, 101, 122
Lyman, Amasa 112, 120, 121, 122, 125, 129, 130
Lyman, Don Carlos (Eliza's son), 122
Lyman, F. M. (Amasa's son), 130
Lyman, Mathew J. (gr. gr. grandson), 104

M

Mountain Meadow Massacre, 125
Majors, Alexander, 75
Malachi (Old Testament), 58
Marsh, Thomas B., 77, 79, 80, 90, 92, 93
Mexican War, 56
Missouri legislature, 82, 87, 96
Missouri Compromise, 62
Missouri constitution, 48
Mitchell, Augustus, 119
Mob Manifesto, 46, 47
Morley, Isaac, 15, 31, 78, 79, 80
Moses (Old Testament), 106, 107
M'Lelland, William, 33, 45, 89

N

Nathanael (Old Testament), 5, 54, 106
Nicene Creed, 4

O

Oak City (Utah; settled in), 124

P

Painesville (Ohio; comforts of), 6, 70, 72
Palestine, 64
Partridge, Caroline (Eliza's daughter), 127
Partridge, Caroline, 21, 44, 95, 112, 117, 121, 122, 123, 124, 127, 129
Partridge, Clisbee, 21
Partridge, Edward grave marker, 103, 104
Partridge, Edward (list of financial losses), 94
Partridge, Edward Jr., 16, 21, 43, 106, 120, 123, 129, 130, 131, 132, 133
Partridge, Eliza, 21, 69, 70, 71,73, 77, 82, 97, 108, 109, 111, 112, 117, 120, 121, 122, 123, 124, 123, 127, 129
Partridge, Eliza Marie (Lydia's granddaughter), 129

Partridge, Emily (Edward Jr.'s daughter), 132
Partridge, Emily, 21, 39, 44, 47, 48, 97, 103, 108, 109, 110, 111, 112, 117, 118, 120, 122, 123, 125, 126, 127, 129
Partridge family, 13, 57, 64, 72,108, 125, 128, 130, 133
Partridge, Harriet, 15, 21, 97, 104, 105
Partridge, James Harvey, 8
Partridge, Jemima, 6, 7, 14
Partridge, Lydia (Lydia's daughter), 21, 120, 124, 125, 127
Partridge, Mary Aloha (Edward Jr.'s daughter), 131
Partridge, William, 6, 14
Patten, David, 63, 90
Petersen, Ziba, 2, 9
Phelps, W.W., 10, 15, 33, 36, 45, 46, 47, 50, 51, 69, 70, 76, 89, 90
Pilate, Pontius, 44, 51
Polygamy, 109, 110
Pony Express, 75
Pool, James, 122
Pratt, Parley P., 2, 3, 9, 51, 53, 63, 80, 81, 89

R

Refiner's fire, 58, 59
Revolutionary War, 7
Reynolds, George, 111
Rigdon, Sidney, 1, 5, 9, 10, 15, 26, 34, 35, 38, 44, 53, 75, 88, 107, 112

S

Sacred Grove, 4
Sessions, Perrigrine, 77
Slavery (in Missouri), 61, 65
Smith, Emma, 109, 110, 111
Smith, Hyrum, 90, 95, 101, 102
Smith, Joseph, 1, 3, 4, 5, 6, 9, 10, 15, 16, 19, 24, 25, 26, 27, 28, 29, 32, 33, 34, 36, 39, 40, 44, 45, 50, 51, 54, 59, 60, 63, 64, 70, 71, 78, 79, 81, 88, 90, 92, 93, 95, 97, 98, 101, 102, 106, 108, 109, 110, 112, 127

Smith, Joseph Sr., 17
Smith, Lucy Mack, 110
Smith, Walter W. (RLDS), 55, 56
Smoot, A. O., 130
Society of Friends (Quakers), 51
Solomon (Old Testament), 33
Soviet Union, 72

T

Taylor, John, 5
Temple lot sale (Jackson County), 122, 123
Tithing, 90
Trinity, 7
Twelve Apostles, 60
Twelve Tribes, 26

W

Whitlock, Harvey, 45
Whitmer, David, 89
Whitmer, John, 15, 45, 89, 90
Whitmer, Peter, 2, 9, 45
Whitney, Newell K., 16, 102
Whitney, Orson, 55
Wight, Lyman, 45, 50, 62, 95
Woodruff, Wilford, 5, 54, 60

Y

Young, Brigham, 5, 54, 60, 90, 97, 98, 107, 111, 112, 117, 122
Young, Edward Partridge (Emily's son), 117, 123

Z

Zion, 13, 14, 20, 23, 24-28, 30, 32-34, 36-40, 51, 53, 59, 61, 63, 65, 72, 79, 89, 90, 97, 98, 102, 107, 108, 128
Zion's Camp (March), 59, 60, 64, 76

WHAT CAUSED THE CONFLICT?

Although the causes of friction between the Latter-day Saints and other settlers were complicated and confused, historians have identified some of their major points of difference:

Land	The Latter-day Saints and other settlers were competing for the same cheap land to settle on.
Slavery	Most Mormons were non-slave holders in a slave state.
Indians	The Mormons tried to befriend and convert the Indians; others feared and distrusted them.
Politics	Many of the original settlers feared that the Mormons numerous enough to take political control of the county.
Economics	The Church store was viewed as competition by some.
Religion	Latter-day Saint beliefs in modern revelation and living offensive to many of their neighbors.
Mormon attitudes	Mormon cooperation and enthusiasm for building Zion some others as clannishness and self-righteousness.
Culture	The Mormons were mostly from the Northern and the nation, while most Missourians were from the S customs, ideas, and lifestyles were different.

Misunderstanding, Conflict, Compromi[se]

Mormon Refugees in Clay County 1833-1836

▲▶▼ **Displays in the LDS Visitors Center**, Independence, Mo., also on a portion of the original temple lot site, attempt to explain the conflict between Mormons and western Missouri residents in early 1830s.

ZION IN MISSOURI

Mormon Ideals on the Frontier
1831-1839

Why did the Mormons come here? The Missouri frontier is the site of Zion for the early members of The Church of Jesus Christ of Latter-day Saints. It was the land designated by the Prophet Joseph Smith, where they would build a new region based on righteous living and unselfish cooperation in accordance with the restored gospel of Jesus Christ. More than 5000 Latter-day Saints took part in this ambitious effort.

What happened to these plans? The dream of an ideal society clashed with the harsh reality of frontier life in Missouri in these times period of violent years. The Mormons left, but their experience here deepened their commitment to the Zion ideals that would bear fruit in other times and places.

◀▼ **Temple lot site in Jackson County, Mo. (Independence)** holds much history for all Latter-day Saints and particularly the family of Edward Partridge. This site was sold by Lydia Partridge in 1848 and was later acquired by the Church of Christ, "Hedrekites."

◀ **A temple of the Reorganized Church of Jesus Christ of Latter-day Saints** now occupies a section of original 63.4 acres encompassing temple site.

◀▼Sacred ground for Mormons at temple lot site in Far West, Caldwell County, Mo. It was here that Edward Partridge and his family thought they could live in peace in a county set aside for the saints. Future events would prove otherwise.

Cemetery markers for ▶David Whitmer and ▶Oliver Cowdery in Richmond, Mo. area. Both men, witnesses to the testimony found in the preface of the Book of Mormon, were excommunicated in difficult Missouri period. Edward was one of a minority of leaders who remained steadfast during this period to Joseph and the Restored Church.

◀▼ **Reminders of the exodus west** which widow Lydia Partridge and all members of the Partridge family made to Utah.

MORMON PIONEER TRAIL

The last mountain pass on the Mormon Pioneer Trail, near the end of a dreary thousand-mile trek from the Missouri River to the Great Salt Lake Valley, can be seen northwest from this point. Thankfully called, by the first company of Pioneers, "Last Mountain." It was later known as Little Mountain. From Big Mountain, 10 miles northeast, the weary travelers caught their first glimpse of the valley. They crossed the Little Mountain pass and descended into Emigration Canyon, from which they entered their Promised Land on July 24, 1847 under the leadership of Brigham Young. About 2,000 other settlers arrived in the Salt Lake Valley the same year.

In all, more than 80,000 Mormon emigrants followed this old trail before the coming of the railroad in 1869. Of these, approximately 6,000 lie buried along the way in unmarked graves.

The first road down Parley's Canyon was opened in 1850 by Parley P. Pratt, but after a short time fell into disuse. About 15 years later it was reopened as the main eastern gateway to the Salt Lake Valley.

·UTAH STATE DEPT. OF HIGHWAYS·

SACRED TO THE MEMORY OF
OLIVER COWDERY
WITNESS
TO THE BOOK OF MORMON AND TO THE TRANSLATION THEREOF BY THE GIFT AND POWER OF GOD.
BORN 3RD OCTOBER, 1806, WELLS, RUTLAND CO. VERMONT.
DIED 3RD MARCH 1850, RICHMOND, RAY CO. MISSOURI.
HE WAS THE SCRIBE OF THE TRANSLATION AS IT FELL FROM THE LIPS OF JOSEPH SMITH THE PROPHET.
HE COPIED THE ORIGINAL MANUSCRIPT FOR THE PRINTER'S USE AND WAS PROOF-READER OF THE FIRST EDITION.
HE WAS THE FIRST PERSON BAPTIZED IN THE LATTER-DAY DISPENSATION OF THE GOSPEL: AND WAS ONE OF THE SIX MEMBERS OF THE CHURCH OF JESUS CHRIST AT IT'S ORGANIZATION, ON THE SIXTH DAY OF APRIL, A.D. 1830, AT FAYETTE, SENECA CO. NEW YORK. THOUGH SEPARATED FROM IT FOR A TIME, HE RETURNED TO THE CHURCH.
HE DIED FIRM IN THE FAITH.
THIS MONUMENT HAS BEEN RAISED IN HIS HONOR BY HIS FELLOW-BELIEVERS: AND ALSO TO COMMEMORATE THE TESTIMONY OF THREE WITNESSES, THE TRUTH OF WHICH THEY MAINTAINED TO THE END OF THEIR LIVES.
OVER A MILLION CONVERTS THROUGHOUT THE WORLD HAVE ACCEPTED THEIR TESTIMONY AND REJOICE IN THEIR FIDELITY.

DEDICATED
1911

OLIVER COWDERY

Utah Historic Site

EDWARD PARTRIDGE, JR. HOUSE

This sandstone house was built by a local contractor for Edward Partridge, Jr., in 1871. Partridge moved to Utah with his mother and other family members in 1848. His father, who died in 1840, was the first bishop of the LDS Church. Edward was extensively involved in the LDS Church, fulfilling two missions, serving as bishop of Fillmore and later as president of the Utah (Provo) Stake. Partridge also served in the Territorial Legislature and was a member of the State Constitutional Convention of 1895. He moved to Provo in the late 1880's, where he lived until his death in 1900.

Marker placed in 1988

Division of State History

▲**Plaque on front of house** commemorates Edward, his leadership and pioneer spirit, on the frontier of mid 1800s.

▶ This is the sturdy, comfortable home, **fashioned out of native stone**, that Edward Partridge Jr. lived in at Fillmore, Utah.

Grave marker for **Lydia Partridge** in Fillmore, Utah.

Portrait of **Edward Partridge**.

▲Marker for **Edward Partridge Sr.** (first bishop) is in Nauvoo, Illinois. It was placed Aug. 30, 1997.

◀Marker for **Edward Partridge Jr.** is in Provo, Utah.

MAP 1

MAP 2

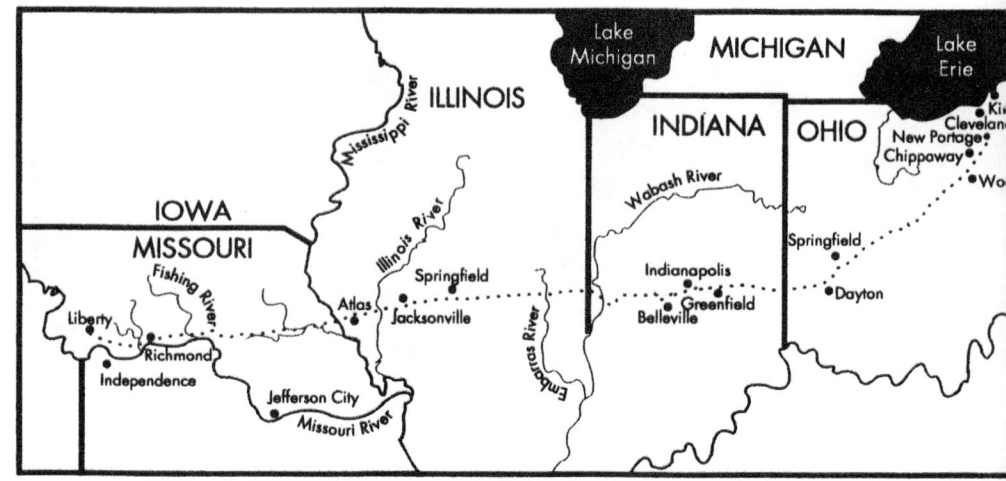

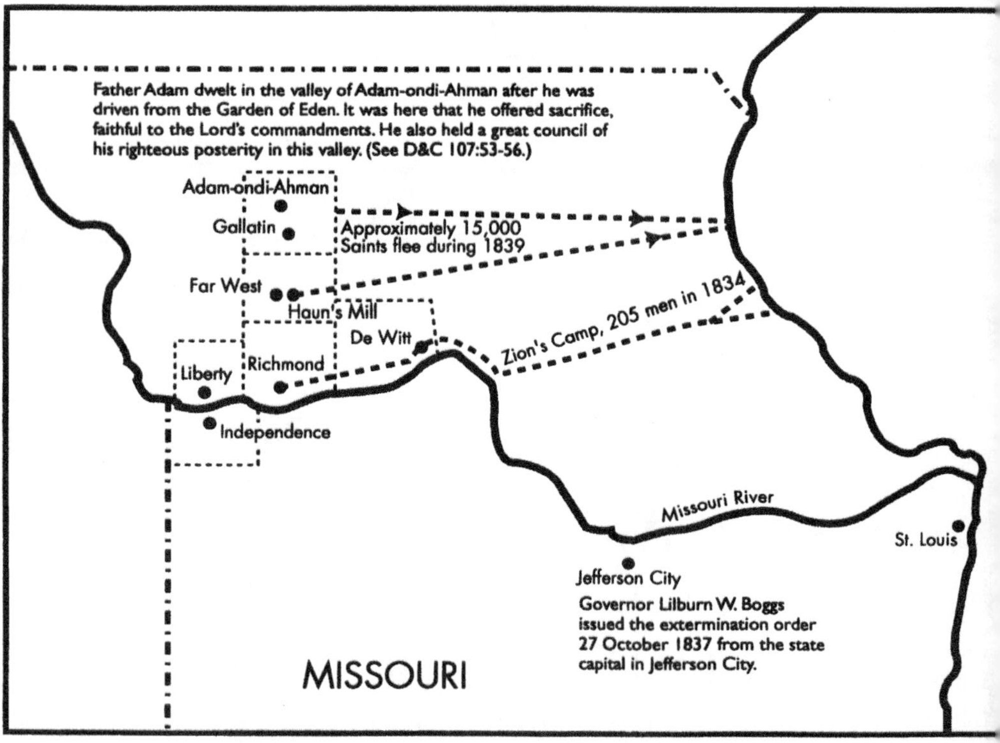

The movements of the Saints during the Missouri difficulties (map adapted from Carter Eldredge Grant, *I Saw Another Angel Fly* [Salt Lake City: Deseret Book Co., 1959], p. 159)

MAP 3

Map showing Iowa, Missouri, and Illinois with locations including Montrose, Nauvoo, Carthage, Warsaw, Quincy, St. Louis, Adam-ondi-Ahman, Gallatin, Far West, Haun's Mill, Liberty, Richmond, Independence, Kaw, and counties Daviess, Caldwell, Ray, Clay, Jackson. Indian Territory to the west. Distance noted: Independence to Kirtland 850 miles. Mississippi River and Missouri River shown.

Jackson County Events

1831

Jan	Missionaries to the Lamanites arrive in Independence
Jul 20	Place of Zion revealed
Jul	Colesville Saints arrive in Jackson County

1831

Aug 3	Independence Temple site dedicated

1833

Nov-Dec	Expulsion from Jackson County to Clay County

Clay County Events

1834

Jun	Zion's Camp in Missouri

1836

Spring	Church leaders in Missouri look for permanent Mormon settlements
Jun 29	Clay county citizens ask Mormons to leave
Dec 29	Caldwell & Daviess

Caldwell & Daviess County Events

1836

Summer	Settlement of Far West

1838

May	Settlement of Adam-ondi-Ahman
Jun	DeWitt settled
Mar 14	Prophet settles in Far West
Aug 6	Election day battle at Gallatin
Oct 25	Battle of Crooked River
Oct 27	Gov. Bogg's "etermination order"
Oct 30	Haun's Mill massacre
Oct 31	Joseph and Church leaders taken prisoner

1839

Feb	Church members flee Missouri

Events in Kirtland

1831

Feb	Joseph Smith arrives in Kirtland

1834

May	Zion's Camp leaves Kirtland

1835

Feb	Quorums of 12 and 70 called

1836

Mar 27	Kirtland Temple dedicated

1837

Jan 12	Joseph flees Kirtland
Jul-Oct	Kirtland Camp journeys to Missouri

Events in Nauvoo

1839

Apr 22	Joseph Smith arrives in Quincy
Apr 30	Joseph Smith negotiates land purchase in Iowa and Illinois
Jul 22	Great day of healing in Nauvoo and Montrose

1841

Apr 6	Cornerstones of Nauvoo Temple laid

1842

Mar 17	Relief Society founded
May	Governor Boggs shot, Joseph Smith blamed

1844

Jan	Joseph Smith begins campaign for president of the United States
Spring	Warsaw Signal begins anti-Mormon articles
Jun 7	First and only edition of Nauvoo Expositor published
Jun 27	Joseph and Hyrum murdered in Carthage